Theology

Polity's *Why It Matters* series

In these short and lively books, world-leading
thinkers make the case for the importance
of their subjects and aim to inspire a
new generation of students.

Helen Beebee & Michael Rush, *Philosophy*
Robert Eaglestone, *Literature*
Lynn Hunt, *History*
Tim Ingold, *Anthropology*
Neville Morley, *Classics*
Alexander B. Murphy, *Geography*
Geoffrey K. Pullum, *Linguistics*
Graham Ward, *Theology and Religion*

Graham Ward

———————

Theology and Religion

Why It Matters

polity

First published in 2019 by Polity Press

Polity Press
65 Bridge Street
Cambridge CB2 1UR, UK

Polity Press
101 Station Landing
Suite 300
Medford, MA 02155, USA

ISBN-13: 978-1-5095-2969-8
ISBN-13: 978-1-5095-2970-4 (pb)

A catalogue record for this book is available from the British Library.

Library of Congress Cataloging-in-Publication Data

Names: Ward, Graham, 1955- author.
Title: Theology and religion : why it matters / Graham Ward.
Description: Cambridge, UK ; Medford, MA : Polity Press, 2019. | Series: Why it matters series | Includes bibliographical references and index.
Identifiers: LCCN 2018035724 (print) | LCCN 2018049751 (ebook) | ISBN 9781509529728 (Epub) | ISBN 9781509529698 (hardback) | ISBN 9781509529704 (pbk.)
Subjects: LCSH: Religion--Study and teaching. | Theology--Study and teaching.
Classification: LCC BL41 (ebook) | LCC BL41 .W37 2019 (print) | DDC 200.7--dc23
LC record available at https://lccn.loc.gov/2018035724

Typeset in 11 on 15 Sabon by Servis Filmsetting Ltd, Stockport, Cheshire
Printed and bound in the UK by CPI Group (UK) Ltd, Croydon

For further information on Polity, visit our website: politybooks.com

For 'Polly' Hardman,
my grandmother

Contents

Acknowledgements

When I was around eight and staying with my grandmother, she took me to 'town' by a different route. Usually we walked to the bus stop. But on this morning she walked me past the greyhound track, where bets were laid on 'dog-nights' on hounds that chased an electronic 'rabbit', and into Peele Park. From there we could walk along Chapel Street and into the centre of Manchester. At the far end of Peele Park, on a hill, stood the University of Salford. The buildings were in a grand, ornate style, built from the same red brick as most of the Victorian slums around it. I stared up at the monumental sight as she clutched my hand. 'One day,' she said, 'if you work hard at school, then maybe you'll come to a place like this.' Although winning a scholarship to continue her education, my grandmother had had to leave school at twelve to help feed and

Acknowledgements

clothe the large number of her younger siblings. The school leaving age rose in 1918, but both my parents also had to leave school at fourteen. So I was the first in my generation to go to university, and the only one of a family of four boys to do so. Later, living with my grandmother, she became the prime force behind my 'staying on'. I owe everything to her for what and where I am today. She saw me go to Cambridge and eventually return to my first Professorial Chair at Manchester (where I lived with her again until her death). I dedicate this book to her memory, and to all those who dream big in deprived conditions.

I would also like to thank the series editor, Pascal Porcheron, for the chance to write this small book and my copy-editor, Justin Dyer, for making my English more accessible and introducing me to the wonderful word 'septillion'.

Introduction

To embark on the study of theology and religion is to undertake an exploration into what we have become and what we are, currently, as human beings. That may sound strange – 'currently' – but we have evolved through the animal chain and our evolution has not stopped. We may well be on the cusp of becoming a different kind of species altogether as 'superintelligence' and Artificial Intelligence (AI) materialize – as we'll see. But our animal (and even plant) lineages remain. As we'll also see, there is some discussion at the moment as to whether other animals can be called 'religious' or behave in certain circumstances in ways that might be termed 'religious'. But it is human beings who have developed rites and liturgies. It is human beings who have responded to their experience of the world in ways that form articulated beliefs in the divine, and

1

have developed those beliefs into systems passed down through hundreds of generations. It is human beings who have written the myths, the legends, and collected the ancient wisdoms. They composed the ancient songs, and recorded the testimonies to unprecedented events, deemed to be historical, out of which sacred books and holy Scriptures emerged. These writings have been handed down, copied by scribes in antique libraries, taught, memorized, translated, and disseminated throughout the world. So vital have these texts become, so vivid are the stories, that they compose the bedrock of many of our human civilizations, having an agency of their own well outside the institutions of worship. It is human beings who have built the churches, mosques, and temples, devised the orders of hallowed offices, populated them with priesthoods, and made them bearers of social authority and cultural power. The study of theology and religion is, then, as much a study of what it is to be human as it is a study of what the word 'God' might mean.

This book will explain and illustrate that statement, at a time when the predictions of secularism have floundered and religion is (again) a prominent player in the public realms of every continent in the world bar Antarctica. But perhaps it always was; and always will be. Perhaps those sets of feelings and intimations we call 'religious' are much older than being human and will still exist when our species fossilizes, like so many other *Homo* species in the past.

So let the journey commence.

The Zagros Mountains are a thousand miles of pleated rock along the edge of Iran, northern Iraq, and southern Turkey. They are often snowcapped and still active glacially. Close to the border with Turkey there's an impressive cave. Tall and wide, it's a dark mouth in the rock face visible for miles. The surrounding area is lush, with green valleys, old olive trees, and pastoral farming between sheer cliffs and precipitous gorges. It's a tranquil place, but it has generated a lot of contestation among archaeologists. The Kurdish people who live in the area are no newcomers to warfare. Only the fighting among the archaeologists is not political.

Archaeologists have known of the Shanidar cave since the 1920s though it was .known to local shepherds and had been a shelter in guerrilla warfare far longer than that. Then, in 1957, the skeletal remains of several Neanderthal bodies dating from 35,000 to 65,000 years old were uncovered in an archaeological excavation below what today creates the floor of the cave. One middle-aged man was found in a trench in the rock floor buried in a foetal position with the skeleton of a baby beneath him and the skeletons of two women above him. The arrangement appeared organized around clan relationships, expressive of both life processes and death. There were other burials in the same cave (and later human burials from around 11,000 years ago). The arrangement was not accidental; archaeologists call it 'intentional', like fire-pits and stone axes.

The most contentious aspect of the discovery were the pollen spores that surrounded the man. The early interpretation for this was that the funeral ceremony involved gifts of flowers. In many parts of the world the dead are often commemorated with fruits and flowers. But such burial customs had never been associated with Neanderthals. So were the pollen spores blown in the wind funnelling down the Great Zab river throughout its stormy winters? Perhaps they were carried on the hoofs of animals that later used the cave for shelter or even on the feet of earlier archaeologists and their team of field-workers? Whatever the answer to the questions that arose, here was evidence of some kind of religious culture from a species of *Homo* that lived before human beings. And the evidence was increasingly supported by the discovery of many more Neanderthal burial sites across Europe.

Introduction

There's no way we can reconstruct such a religion. The burials (there are ten of them in the cave) reveal complex levels of social organization and relations of respect for the corpse. The rites that accompanied such burials are the stuff of historical novelists, and any notion of an afterlife is guesswork. But what the contents of the cave reveal is a sensitive response to being alive; a conscious and reflective response. For what we do with our dead, and how we think about what death means, speaks loudly about our conscious understanding of life. It speaks about the values we place on living in communities and the relationships fostered within those communities. And neither these communities nor the intimacies they nurture can be isolated from the wider ecological conditions that make them possible: the weather we endure, the landscape we tread, the water, plants, and animals that sustain us. Our environment matters; we're part of it. Where death is respected, so is the life that was once lived, the person who lived it, and the collective memories that life generated. How far back these intentional burials go archaeologists are still trying to fathom, but what is clear is that various hominids (and *Homo sapiens* among them) respond to their environments religiously, with respect. They don't just labour to survive and tame them, they assert a need to flourish creatively and imaginatively. Outside the cave at Shanidar, archaeologists found evidence for the domestication of animals. This is more than just settlement; it's cultivation. At other Neanderthal sites, pendants have been found, even a bone flute. These earlier forms of being human fashioned what was given to them into the civilizations whose ruins we now preserve so carefully.

And if we can ever posit an origin for religion, it's here – with that creative and imaginative flourishing that binds conscious and articulate creatures to the land, to the sky, to the wildlife, to that which grows or can be made to grow, to that which falls to the ground and dies, and to that which is born or returns again seasonally. The destruction of our environments, then, also raises religious responses. For we are sentient, as all organisms are sentient to a certain extent. We respond to the world that encompasses us; and religion is integral to that response. It is the wakeful consciousness that we are here, we know not how and we know not why, blown by solar winds from the dust of stars.

This raises questions that we will explore further when we consider human uniqueness, the possibilities of other animals expressing religious responses, and the current ecological crisis. Can religion ever be erased? Is it not a perennial part of being alive; of being conscious that we are alive? Is it not part of our continual need to understand our experience of the world? What I'll be arguing throughout this short book is that we human beings don't simply *make* that experience meaningful, we forage within ourselves for *why* it is meaningful.

These questions and their implications are basic to the study of theology and religion at university level. Whether treating myths of Eden or doctrines of sin, the rites of shamans, the subtleties of a Sanskrit phrase, or near-death experiences, what religion is, why it emerges, how it has captured (and still captures) the dreams, hopes, ambitions, and aspirations of billions of people over thousands of years – all these galvanize the curiosity of those wishing to study this subject. In its different ways, with its different texts and its eyes on different practices of devotion, the study of theology and religion pursues a set of interrelated questions fundamental to all the sciences – human, social, and physical. Why are we here? What does it mean? What is it to be conscious that we are alive?

But before we proceed we need to take a step back; because the study of theology and religion is not new, and its purpose has changed. Its intellectual purpose in contemporary society is not always understood.

Introduction

The study of theology in universities goes right back to the origin of universities themselves – in twelfth-century Bologna, Paris, and Oxford. There were so-called *magisters* teaching Christian theology in Oxford from the arrival of the Augustinian canons on the site of what is now Christ Church Cathedral. The records tell of one Roger Pullen teaching theology in 1123, *before* the University of Oxford was founded. And prior to that, theology was taught in abbey and cathedral schools. Here priests were trained and congregations were instructed in the Christian faith.

And Christian theology is not unique here. Instruction in religious beliefs was part of everyone's education in every society; for religion *defined* that society, giving it an identity and a history. Jewish teaching was organized around Houses of Study (*beth midrashim*) from the destruction of the Temple in Jerusalem in 70 CE, and these can trace their roots back further into the second century BCE. From the Semitic *midrash* we get the Arabic *madrasah* (the Muslim centres of teaching). The study of the Vedas in the Indian traditions goes back even earlier, to the first millennium BCE, when texts were collected, with commentaries upon those texts, and taught orally by the Brahmans. So, from the moment when religion becomes organized and its social institutions are formed, its teachings (what we call theology) have always been recognized as crucial to 'hand on'. That 'handing on' is what is understood by the word 'tradition'. Today we might perceive that the purpose of tradition is to preserve the past – like those ancient tiny life forms trapped in amber. But traditions are not necessarily conserving and conservative. Traditions were once conceived as being orientated towards the future, instructing the generations to come. We'll understand why when we come to look at the relationship between religion and power, authority, and politics more generally. Every class of those who belonged and joined a particular community was taught in its religious beliefs and practices, its gods, and the devotion due to those gods. If people couldn't read or write, there were the sculptures, the buildings, the paintings, the music, and the festivals that instructed them to respect things divine.

The Old Ways

The modern university began to take shape in the Prussian capital of Berlin at the beginning of the nineteenth century. Because Lutheran clergy were appointed by the state and regarded themselves as civil servants, theology was one of the four main faculties of that modern university – with law, medicine, and what were known as the 'sciences' as the other three. The theology was Christian and, indeed, there's a misperception even today that 'theology' means 'Christian theology'. Which it doesn't. Back then, however, it did; or, more precisely, it meant 'Protestant Christian theology'. The study of theology provided the basis for the training of clerics, church administrators, and teachers.

This Prussian organization of the study of theology continued to inform the way the academic discipline was taught for over 150 years – not only in the West, but also in those continents (Asia and Africa, for example) that it colonized The basis of the syllabus I was taught at Cambridge in the 1980s still retained much of the shape inherited from the Protestant study of Christianity.

It has been said before: the past is another country. But we need to pay this country a visit in order to allay any number of misperceptions that potential students might have about studying theology and religion in universities today. Because in the past such a study was quite a different quest, conducted through quite a different landscape, and in pursuit of quite different ends. Very few students today take this subject at a university because they wish to enter some ordained ministry. And a state's civil service is drawn from a wider pool of applicants, many of whom have not been educated at university. Some of the most popular courses being currently taught are on 'New Atheism' or shamanism or decolonization.

In my day, the study of theology meant: a grounding in the biblical languages (Hebrew, Greek, and as many others as you could cope with, from Ugaritic to Syriac); the study of biblical texts; texts by the Early Church Fathers from the second to the thirteenth centuries; church history; systematic theology; philosophical theology; and Christian ethics. Sometimes more practical courses were offered on pastoral theology, Christian liturgy, and homiletics (sermon writing and delivery). A nod was given to current trends by adding a text or offering lecture courses on 'Feminist Theology' or 'Black Theology'; or including a course on the study of interpretation (hermeneutics) within philosophical theology. If the word 'religion' was used, it was always prefaced with the word 'revealed'. 'Revealed religion' referred to those beliefs and practices based on revelation – God having revealed Himself (and it was certainly a He) through Jesus Christ.

The study of theology today is radically different. Why it's different is important to understand because I will be arguing throughout (somewhat controversially) for the singleness of the discipline of theology and religion; the intellectual advantages of studying both subjects in tandem. Changes in the UK, where I teach, followed in the wake of the reorganization of academic departments in universities and new student demands. Before then, the study of theology was entirely separate from the study of religion, and each had its own way of handling religious beliefs. The separation remains within more traditional American universities (Harvard, Yale, and Princeton, for example), where the departments of religion are institutionally distinct from their divinity schools.

The study of religion has its own history in higher education, its own approaches, databases, and intellectual societies. It was (and is) shaped around introductions to world faiths; the comparative study of two of these faiths through appropriate texts and languages; the philosophy of religion; the sociology of religion; the psychology of religion; the anthropology of religion; and the study of ritual. It related itself to the social sciences, while theology was still classed under the ancient tradition of the liberal arts, as one of the humanities.

Justification for the division of theology and religion was (and still is in many universities across the world) defended along the lines of the 'insider perspective' (theology) and the 'outsider perspective' (religion). So those studying theology were insiders (or believers) learning more about the faith tradition to which they were already committed and even being professionally trained for an office in that tradition. Studying religion, on the other hand, viewed various belief systems objectively, as cohesive collections of prescribed teachings (or ideologies). 'Ideologies' can be understood as the power of interrelated ideas exercised socially and politically. Students of religion studied the phenomenon of different religions as sets of social and cultural practices that formed the way people think through specific ideas and values – whether Mormons in Utah or Sufis in Istanbul, Catholics in Guatemala or Snake-Handlers in Texas. They adopted methods of investigation such as ethnography and comparative mythology from the anthropologists; the analysis of statistics from the sociologists working with officially gathered data; analytical logic from the philosophers; and theories of ego development from the psychologists.

I would argue that the separation of the study of religion from the study of theology encouraged walls to be built separating the intellectual disciplines, thus encouraging a reductive division between insiders and outsiders. There was revealed religion, on the one hand, and 'methodological atheism', on the other. But even before change came about in the UK through enforced economic circumstances, the walls separating these two studies proved very distorting and unworkable. For the non-believer it was difficult to imagine, for example, the emotional power that comes with hearing or reading a text regarded by a particular faith as sacred. The text has been recited, memorized, translated, over many centuries by communities nurtured and shaped by its phrasing and resonances. Its public reading, its vocalization, carries with it aeons of association and deep, mythical sensibilities. On the other hand, it was difficult for the believer to recognize that sacred text *as* a text, *as* a piece of writing like any other piece of writing, or even like the very best pieces of writing we call 'literature'. The language of the text, whether ancient Hebrew, Koranic Arabic, or Sanskrit, is time-bound so that words change in their meaning. Texts can be dissected grammatically, their layers dated, their different authorships detected, their commonalities with other texts held sacred charted. And yet . . .

The insider's faith commitment is not hermetically sealed from the social, economic, and political circumstances in which they live. A believer is also a member of any number of other forms of society, and affected as those other members of society are affected. Furthermore, no religious faith is monolithic. Judaism, Christianity, Islam, and Hinduism are lived and practised very differently in other parts of the globe, and there are various sects within all of them. So articulations of the beliefs involved in that faith take on the cultural colouring of their time and situation. A world faith is not simply a set of its key teachings or doctrines. It is also practices of piety embedded in specific times and particular locations. For example, in the aftermath of the Jewish holocaust, Christian theology in the West reassessed the continuities between Judaism and Christianity and the Jewish character of Jesus Christ. As empires and colonies came to an end, then indigenous and naturalized peoples began to recognize the European nature of the faiths that had come to them through the various missions. In South Africa, a Christian theology that some had used to support apartheid began to be seen as a Calvinist heritage; a heritage that needed to be rethought so a Christian faith more in keeping with its African location might be developed.

Similarly, the outsider's atheism (methodological or otherwise) is not hermetically sealed either. In any ethnographic examination of the new spiritualisms that are prominent in contemporary Brazil, the anthropologist will need to have engaged with the relevant languages (Spanish, its Creole variants, and the indigenous languages of the Amazon), read the colonial histories of the country, understood the waves of Pentecostal missionizing, and observed the prominent gender divisions in any particular group in order to 'see' through the eyes of its practitioners. Only in this way can the ethnographer appreciate how sense is being made of what the devotees are doing, and with what social and cultural implications. There will be no understanding or approach to an understanding that does not involve moving closer to what the insider believes and experiences, and takes that into account.

So the insider/outsider perspectives lie on a spectrum of possibilities between engagement and an objectivity that can never be as objective as it hopes. Perspectives are forever changing as circumstances change. Alliances can be forged between various places to stand, observe, and reflect within that spectrum. Both insider and outsider positions lie within complex social and cultural networks, some of which are not religious. So contemporary ecological movements, for example, draw religious and non-religious commitment to a common concern with the environment and the way human beings have significantly impacted upon the planet in our current geological age, the Anthropocene.

So, while seemingly pure theologies continue, unadulterated by secularism, other more liberal theologies reach out into the social and cultural sciences and the debates between insiders and out-siders have grown increasingly noisy. The debates still continue, but there is much to learn from each other. The study of theology *and* religion offers the best provision for what I take to be one of the core purposes of studying the subject at university level: developing a greater understanding of why religions remain globally important *today*.

For the Times They Are a-Changin'

With the new economic, political, and cultural reali-ties of the late twentieth and the early twenty-first centuries, the student body and their interests were changing. Demand arose for courses engaging with new global circumstances and the big questions, and this brought about a change in the purpose driving the study of both theology and religion. Questions were raised about the place of the study of theology, particularly Western Christian understandings of it, in the secular university. Questions were also being

asked about the study of religions. The comparative method of studying them came under attack
as the use of the word 'religion' as a common basis
for comparisons was challenged. 'Religion' comes
from the Latin word 'to bind' and was introduced
into the West to describe other devotional practices
only in the sixteenth century: the Age of Discovery
(*and* colonizing expansion). There is no similar
word in Judaism, Islam, or Hinduism. This is not
a word they use to describe themselves. Was not,
then, even the classing of these faiths and practices as 'religions' an illegitimate act of Eurocentric
imposition? The very word 'Hinduism' as a term
covering a variety of Asian practices of worship was
a nineteenth-century invention.

In universities, syllabi began to shape-shift.
Chapters 3 and 4 outline just two of the major shifts:
towards studying the relationship between religion
and international politics (Chapter 3) and between
religion and science (Chapter 4). The response from
departments was, in the main, twofold. First, they
embraced the pluralism of theologies so that the
term 'theologian' is regaining its non-Christian
association. It's an ancient Greek word in origin
and was used from antiquity to describe poets and
writers as various as Orpheus, Homer, Plato, and
Moses. It referred to a writer who was divinely

inspired. Secondly, departments took up better tools to engage studying religious faiths from an international perspective. Models of analysis and examination from the study of religion became crucial.

Most departments of theology and religion today are still working their way towards a new sense of their purpose in the contemporary university: developing religious literacy as part of a wider education for all citizens in our current globalized situation. It is an education much needed when so many have mistakenly accepted that religion will increasingly disappear (the secularization thesis). That has certainly not been the case, as we will see in the next chapter.

Meanwhile, as I have said, there are intellectual benefits from studying theology *and* religion together. They are not the same and their approaches differ (in brief: the inside/believer perspective and the outsider/agnostic perspective). But in their common pursuit of religious literacy, the study of each adds something substantial to the other. The practice of faith has a very powerful effect upon an individual schooled in its truth. Fanaticism is all too possible, destabilizing national and international orders. The study of religion's attention to the ideological forces at work in a particular faith – forces that mould opinion, behaviour, and emotion – can facilitate a critical distance for a particular faith, raising important questions about its practice and beliefs. However vigorous the conviction, however sacred the text, however forthright the revelation attested to in and through that text, the religionist reminds the theologian that their work is a product of its culture, and as such it is subject to all the strengths and weaknesses of being human. Whatever 'revelation' might mean to a particular faith tradition, it is not a direct and unmediated event. It has a history and a language that are all too human. The tradition can be studied as a cultural science because theologians work with interpretations and translations, and the changes wrought by time. They have no immediate access to either God or Truth, and any claim to such has to be treated with the scepticism we would apply to a pathology. For every true prophet there are crowds of paranoid schizophrenics. And every faith institution (mosque, church, and temple) has its processes of discernment: its trained clerics, its wise men and women, its counsellors and directors who assist in sifting the psychic from the psychotic, the magi from the megalomaniac, the spiritual from the spurious.

Meanwhile, the recognition of a theology's sociological, political, and cultural effects enables the study of religion to appreciate that faith is deeply rooted in what it is to be human. We're back with those Neanderthal graves in the Zagros Mountains. There are depths of being human, of becoming human, that we barely comprehend – if at all. Religion will not be erased – as the Western and colonial theories of secularization supposed – because it plumbs the depths of human dreaming, desire, and conviction, giving it material content through its teachings and practices. And there are far too many sane, well-adjusted, and rational people who espouse a belief in the divine for religion to be glibly dismissed as an illusion to be outgrown. It may have tendencies to be (as Marx believed) 'the opium of the people'; it may grandly distribute placebos for social and economic ills; it may be used to uphold unjust and oppressive political regimes – but then so do commercial consumerism, and the pumping and pulsing that go on in most gyms. Life being the challenge it is, we all find mechanisms for coping. And faith *can* be used as a coping mechanism. No doubt about it. Nevertheless, theologies are composed from religious myths that, however they are interpreted, employed, and redeployed, remain imaginatively very powerful. The religious stories that communities tell themselves, that they tell about themselves, and that make sense of life, have muscular tone and raw, feral intensity. They can capture. They can captivate. They can facilitate magnanimous, self-denying good and appalling evil. As a human species, we have to understand the hold that religion has because it unlocks some of the mysteries of our capabilities – and that is why the study of theology and religion matters.

Conclusion

As Bob Dylan sang, 'the wheel's still in spin', but it seems to me, even outside the UK, that the two distinct approaches of theology and religion are increasingly in conversation. And the students enrolled on courses in theology and religion are part of the development of an imaginative science that brings together philological and historical interests with in-depth examination of sacred texts, of faith as it's practised in different parts of the world, and a wide appreciation of our contemporary cultural conditions: in the physical and medical sciences and in the arts and social sciences. The challenge, and it is a challenge, is the elaboration of an in-depth account of what it is to be human and the role religious belief, traditions, institutions, and rituals play in that account.

Introduction

Around 1265, in the basilica of Santa Sabina in Rome, Thomas Aquinas began to write his famous *Summa Theologica*. The first question is devoted to what kind of a science theology is. Central to his argument is that it is a science that draws upon every other science, because although it treats that which lies beyond human reason, it has to use every form of human reason, practical and speculative, in its task. Does that make it the 'queen of the sciences', as our mediaeval predecessors thought? No. Today, it goes hand in hand with the other sciences (including religious studies) in the pursuit of the truth about what we are and where we came from and why we're here.

1

A Millennial Age

Many students today choose to study theology and religion because they want to understand something about the world they live in; a world in which religion has such a constant media presence. For those in the West who undertake this study, this is a 'Millennial' or 'Generation Y' world: the world as it is experienced by those between the ages of seventeen and twenty-nine or those born between the late 1980s and 2001. Millennial dates are flexible, but the world these individuals have entered is in complex flux and that complexity has to be adapted to and, as much as it possible, regulated. It is a world of red, apocalyptic presentiments and orange, futuristic promises.

It is not the world I was born into where a man or a woman left college and started a profession and worked their way up to as far they aspired or had the talent for or the luck to reach. Many of my generation were upwardly mobile, bought their homes, and could afford to take early retirement. Pensions were secure and secured. With prudence and savings a last stage of life could be planned and, for many, the plans worked out. Mine was a property-owning generation, and even though many were caught in the easy credit available until the banks crashed (2008), many others grew up with a post-war aversion to credit and an obsession with putting aside for a rainy day. My generation sits on stockpiled assets that others will inherit, use well, or squander.

Millennials, by contrast, have no such job security – technological advances move so fast that training and retraining is perpetual, and likewise the skills for employment. There are jobs in the future few of us can guess the shape of and demand for. Millennials will rarely have a single career trajectory. Their savings are thin, their college debts deep, and retirement is a dream at least fifty years in the blue-sky distance. It's a dream that they are not over-convinced they or the human race will ever realize. They scan their social media headlines, sorting the fake from the true, and because they live the globalization that has been creeping up on all of us since colonization, they know they will not be unaffected by a nuclear war in the far-flung east, the rise in sea-levels as the polar ice melts, the depletion of oil resources or the effervescence of Middle Eastern politics. They read the signs of the time well, but their optimism for the future waxes and wanes depending upon whether they get well-paid jobs with prospects or a place on the property ladder or they party with friends. Friends are more important than family. What is uppermost, as far as attainment is concerned, is some stable years of a chosen life-style. And they travel, like their restless *Homo erectus* descendants.

And into this fluid, fast-paced, pop-up mix emerges religion – frequently emotionally frothed like a macchiato, vivacious, and calling attention to itself with its hard-headed, even violent, self-assertiveness. It's not one thing. But it's everywhere. Viral. The situation is not quite as new as some think. The debate still is out on how deep or superficial secularism (often understood as the same as atheism) really is. It's not a world-wide phenomenon. In Britain the decline in church attendance, for example, occurred only in the 1960s and was both paralleled and outrun by the decline in the participation in other institutions, from boy scouts to trade unions and political parties. The situation is new if you believed that Western progress meant the decline and disappearance of religion. Secularism was and remains a bureaucratic ideal. It's a way of governing people by providing a common denominator, a default position: we choose what we want to believe in. It became, for some, a mindset.

Secularism

All university programmes in the study of theology and religion provide a foundational year offering a series of 'Introductions to . . .' that enable students to orientate themselves in the discipline: an introduction to various world faiths, for example; an introduction to the languages of those faiths and their sacred texts; and an introduction to how we approach and interpret both those practices of religious piety in their historical and ritual settings, and the various forms they have taken over the centuries. How we approach and make sense of religious things in theology and religion is often called 'methodology', and in the first year familiarization with any number of 'isms and ologies' is necessary: secularism, atheism, agnosticism, existentialism, on the one hand; ontology, epistemology, phenomenology, mythology, on the other. But 'secularism' is a good place to start because it is often understood as 'anti-religious'. That's not how the 'ism' began and it's not what the French government, with their constitutionally enshrined principle of *laïcité*, believe the enforcement of that principle amounts to. The French government believed they were protecting the public sphere from Roman Catholic bigotry, exclusivism, and preferential privilege. But, as will be increasingly observed, there is a difference between an idea (or, for the French, a policy) and its reception.

The modern development of secularism was born in the West. It's a Western notion primarily, taken up and adapted elsewhere – and often criticized elsewhere for being imperial and Eurocentric. It was born from a particular historical set of circumstances that brought ravaging wars in the late sixteenth and seventeenth centuries that are often labelled 'religious' because positions were consolidated around Catholicism and Protestantism. But the power grabs of princes and the emergence of the nation state, the rise of the bourgeoisie, and the advancement in new technologies (like printing) were all part of a potent cultural cocktail.

The Wars of Religion offer an early insight into the complex affiliations between religion and politics, and the mobilizing power of religious conviction. Somewhere between 3 and 11 million people lost their lives in the Thirty Years War over the Holy Roman Empire (1618–48); between 2 and 4 million people lost their lives in the French Wars of Religion (1562–98); and around 185,000 people lost their lives either in combat or in war-related diseases in the English Civil War (1642–51). Europe had not been so devastated since the Black Death (1346–53).

A separation of church and state was called for as various edicts of toleration were drawn up by governments and came into effect. A new organization of society was needed where religion might withdraw from open view, become interiorized, and be made a personal choice. A new political space was created: the public realm. It was a space increasingly buzzing with the free market in opinion, and legislated by the parliamentary state. It was an ideal; a bureaucratic ideal. It was never fully realized, and there were complex relations between thrones, altars, and elected representatives to governing bodies. But along with the development and increasing acceptance of human rights (for centuries more accurately the rights of *man*), the stability of a new order in Europe was slowly established, taking longer in some countries (like Germany and Italy) than in others (Britain and Holland).

The bureaucratic ideal was first exported to what

is now known as the United States in the eighteenth century. As colonial expansion inflated, it was made quite clear in the territories annexed abroad that their subjugated peoples were neither competent to wield the power of the state nor human enough to be given 'rights'. But that is another story – taught today as part of courses in post-colonialism, world Christianities, and liberation theologies.

As a bureaucratic ideal, secularism sought to foster inclusivity, even multiculturalism. Bigotry and intolerance, however, lay just beneath the legal tarmacking – against Jews, Muslims, Hindus, and Roman Catholics; against people of colour (as if being 'white' wasn't a colour), gays, and women. But the ideal was established and increasingly encoded in civil and sometimes constitutional law. It gained in attraction because it offered what was much needed after the Wars of Religion: social peace. Social peace facilitated nation-building. And to dismiss the benefits of secularism, for the West, would be a little like the reply given in *Monty Python's Life of Brian* to the dissident who demands to know, 'What did the Romans ever do for us?'

But, gradually, as the secularization thesis gained ground after the Second World War, secularism became something more than a bureaucratic ideal. It became a culture in which it was believed that notions of 'God' would be left behind – at least in Western Europe, and most particularly in France. Spain, Italy, and Austria remained somewhat recalcitrant. Despite the First Amendment to the Constitution – 'the United States Constitution prevents Congress from making any law respecting an establishment of religion' – the US has remained a predominantly Christian country. Outside Western Europe, the bureaucratic ideal of secularism gets played out very differently, and not at all securely. When countries like India, Tunisia, Turkey, and Egypt (to name only a few) talk about 'secular government', this is, to employ a phrase by Naser Ghobadzadeh, 'religious secularity'. That is, the government is inclusive with respect to all persons but committed to maintaining the importance of religious opinion in the public sphere.[1]

The Secular Imagination

In becoming more than a bureaucratic ideal, secularism fostered a certain culture in the West. 'Culture' is likely to be another word that the foundational

---

[1] Naser Ghobadzadeh, *Religious Secularity: A Theological Challenge to the Islamic State* (Oxford: Oxford University Press, 2015).

year of any course in the study of theology and religion will examine. If what we call 'society' is a group of people (and we're talking very generally here), then 'culture' can be understood as the way that people express themselves – from the clothes they wear and the films they make, to the practices they develop and perform to the buildings they design. All the practices and the makings involve the use of symbols, though some of the symbolic force involved may now be diluted to the point of not being apparent at all.

When we examine literature or painting or even billboard advertising, it's obvious we are decoding symbols – language, images, colours, and designed depiction. But washing your hands before a meal? At a time of increased awareness of bacterial infection and superbugs, and the ways they can be transmitted, it may now seem like a good hygienic practice. But behind it lies an ancient purification rite of entering a sacred place having bathed first, and a whole set of hidden ideas about dirt and where it belongs. It's a practice that marks the end of one kind of collective activity (labouring), even a certain time of the day, and the start of a very different collective activity (eating). It often demarcates outside activity (in the fields) from inside activity (in the house). We can call it a 'liturgy' because it's bound by certain unspoken rules, values, and social expectations. We are creatures of habit; habit saves space in our short-term memories.

On the other hand, some ways of doing things are evidently and consciously more symbolic – like laying a wreath of poppies at the Cenotaph in Whitehall, London, or welcoming a new neighbour with a gift of bread, salt, and oil (often found in Mediterranean countries), or even dressing up for Halloween.

Religious cultures are rich in liturgical traditions, and flamboyant in their use of symbols. In fact, religious cultures are dependent upon symbols for their identities and continuation: codes of dress, ways of behaving (and not behaving), foods enjoyed (and foods forbidden), their use of water or oil or wine or fruit, and, most prominently, the architectures and furnishings of the sacred buildings where their most important rituals take place. If the Jews have their scrolls, then the Christians have their cross and the Muslims their crescent. I once had a student who told me he learnt most of his understanding of the wide variety of Christian theologies that were possible as an altar server watching the way different priests dressed and approached the celebration of a liturgy like the mass or a baptism. 'Some bowed and kissed, elevated and genuflected. For others it was a more like a lesson in cookery or the hospitable laying out of a meal.' These symbolic activities also serve to mark divisions in the year (with feasts and festivals) and divisions across a lifetime (from initiations of belonging to burial).

If, in the ascendance of secularism, fewer people participated in these religious rites or chose when to participate and when not to, then secularism was not lacking its own symbolic cultures. It invented its own 'liturgies' and its own 'traditions'. Charles Dickens and Victorian Britons cultivated the Christmas most of us are familiar with. They invented most of the foods we associate today (in the northern hemisphere) with Christmas. Much of what goes for the frills and trimmings of Christmas has been driven by commerce and is only loosely now associated with a religious festival in the Christian calendar. There's very little in *A Christmas Carol*, other than the word 'carol' itself, which is religious. But the story has retained a moral tone and features ghosts and spirits of various kinds, even though the cultural imagination behind it is infused with secular humanism.

First-year students are often asked what they consider religious, and the answers can be wide-ranging. The question is a way of getting them to think about what the term might mean and where religion might be found. And it's surprising how, in their responses, its Latin roots (*religare* – to bind; *religio* – an obligation or bond) endure. What they list as religions are not just old traditions like Judaism or new cults like Wicca. Frequently, students respond by viewing nationalism as a religion and being a football supporter as religious. And I could sympathize with those responses.

I grew up in Manchester, almost directly opposite the old training ground for Manchester United, and certainly there was a great deal more excitement, enthusiasm, and sacrificial devotion about Saturdays in the football stadiums than Sunday mornings in the churches. It was an excitement, enthusiasm, and sacrificial devotion to the point of sectarianism: the rivalry between Manchester City and Manchester United in the 1960s and 1970s doesn't come close to their rivalry in the English Premier League today. It spilled over into a rivalry between Catholics and Protestants, itself fostered by a deep division between the Scottish and Irish, on the one hand, and the English-born, on the other. When the two teams were playing each other, then Saturday in town from lunchtime to kick-off and from the final whistle to closing time in the pubs was like something from the War of the Roses. Heat and emotion were generated that seemed to go back centuries before the English Civil War. Yes, for someone who did not grow up through the two world wars – and so nationalism was much more muted – football was a respectable answer to the question 'What counts as a religion?'

The secularized imagination is not, then, deficient in its cultural expression, and the absence of 'God' or the 'gods' need not preclude a set of valued practices (like supporting a football team) from being religious in a general sense. From 26 August 1994, Sunday religious services also had a secular rival in England and Wales: Sunday shopping. So cultural, leisure pursuits forged new practices and new expressions under the secular imagination. God was dead. New atheism was flexing its intellectual and polemical muscles and religion was one option in an open market where now, due to waves of migration, a whole variety of new stalls were appearing, from Bahá'í to religious Nones. The Nones (those professing no religion, though not necessarily atheists in the Richard Dawkins mould) tend to embrace a liberal humanism. Often LBTQ-friendly, ecologically engaged, and sceptical (if not downright worried) about religious experience, the Nones articulate a secularism that itself forms a belief system. Their appearance (and self-identification) is a recognition that 'secularism' too is an ideology. That comes as shock to the cerebral system – because secularism had presented itself, as I said, as a bureaucratic ideal and some default position in human nature. Human beings under secularist thinking were considered to be without religion or a religious disposition of any kind. And this was the destiny of all future human generations – at least according to those theorists of secular progress.

But it was not to be. The Millennials (a number of whom come to study theology and religion because they wish to understand the world in which they live) were born into a world that was radically distinct from the post-Second World War generation in the West. A world where religion didn't just persist, but seemed to aggressively pursue a revenge. Like the famous Freudian notion of the return of all that has been repressed, what is consciously denied and incubated in febrile darknesses of the unconscious surfaces again in nightmarish scenarios of terrorist atrocity. The culture given expression for the Millennials, in this distinctive, globalized world, is religious through and through.

A Millennial Age

Post-Secularism

Some sociologists have started using this term, so it could well crop up in class or discussions. It's not a very precise term. It seems to suggest that 'secularism' is the same the world over, and it's not. There's increasing talk among scholars of 'varieties' of secularism. The US has always been viewed as a Western exception to the secularization thesis. As just one example: a Gallup poll done in 1994 found 72 per cent of Americans believed in angels. This had risen, in 2004, to 78 per cent. That was a high point. In 2016 the poll found it was 72 per cent again. In Europe, as the inventor of secularism, there's no head-count on belief in angels (that I know of). But since 1981 there has been a European Survey of Values with some specific questions asked on belief in God and the afterlife and belonging to an identified religious community. For the last two decades there has been a notable upwards trend in religious beliefs. This is particularly among young people claiming to believe in some notion of a world spirit and an afterlife. Other statistics are also suggestive of an upward turn in what is sometimes referred to as 'spiritual but not religious' or 'believing without belonging'. And certainly there has been a global revival in pilgrimage to holy sites in Europe, the

Middle East, and India. The number of officially registered pilgrims walking across France and Spain to the tomb of St James in Santiago, Compostela, in 1987 was just under 3,000. But there has been a year-on-year increase so that, in 2015, the number of officially registered pilgrims was 262,500. The Alliance of Religions and Conservation in 2011 claimed the number of people visiting just the tomb was 1.5 million. Visitors to Lourdes for the same year were estimated at 8 million.

In the face of these trends, former academic backers of the secularization thesis – that the world is going to become less not more religious as Enlightened progress increases – were, by the late 1990s, having to eat their words. As Martin Rees, the Astronomer Royal, put it in 2002, in a controversial book questioning the ability of the human race to reach the end of the new century: 'Techno-forecasters . . . tend to envisage that changes proceed untrammelled. . . . These presumptions may be as unwarranted as it would have been to downplay the role of religion in international affairs.'[2] Religion had been downplayed – even while the politicization of Islam grew apace following the Iranian Revolution and

[2] Martin Rees, *Our Final Century: Will Civilization Survive the Twenty-First Century? Will the Human Race Survive the Twenty-First Century?* (New York: Random House, 2004), p. 21.

the downfall of the Shah in 1979. And it is not only Islam that has been grabbing international headlines. If we take what was once a Christian term for a radical conservative commitment to key teachings of that faith – fundamentalism – well, there's the Buddhists in Myanmar, Borneo, and Sri Lanka; the Hindu fundamentalists in India; the Jewish fundamentalists in Israel; and Christian fundamentalists in every corner of the globe.

So where does all this leave 'secularism'? After all, it's still a word widely used – most particularly by nation states wishing to maintain neutrality with respect to individual opinion and seeking to be inclusive with respect to all citizens within their borders. It's also widely used by religious institutions that, for one reason or another, like to pitch it as the 'enemy' threatening their ministries and mission. Well, if 'secularism' denotes an attempt to free the public sphere from religious debate and reduce it to the realm of a private, individual right to choose one's beliefs, then the new visibility of religion in the international public sphere points to its failure as a Western, Enlightenment project. The project has come to an end and, as has been seen recently in France, state-sponsored policies of *laïcité* have come under attack as anti-religious ideology and state interference. If 'secularism' denotes some anthropological condition – that human beings are not by nature religious animals, rather they are 'naturally' non-religious and being religious is a personal choice – then that too is questionable.

What is clear is that being secular is no longer a destiny all human beings will arrive at when they mature psychologically and understand the nature of things more clearly (that is, according to what scientists can demonstrate to be the case). We can't simply get some data on Western church, mosque, temple, or synagogue attendance and show an over-all decline. This is certainly an indication of social change, but the question is: what kind of change? As I said earlier with respect to Britain, there has been an equally – in fact, more – dramatic change in all forms of institutional affiliation. People are wary of commitment to institutions and so to institutionalized religion. But some intuition nevertheless persists, such that even Richard Dawkins (that self-appointed zealot of New Atheism) identifies himself as a 'cultural Anglican' and a 'secular Christian'.[3] Indeed, 'Cultural Christian' now has its own Wikipedia entry.

---

[3] Claire Carter, 'Richard Dawkins admits he is a "cultural Anglican"', *Daily Telegraph*, 12 September 2013.

A Millennial Age

The Return of Myth

So what we are left with is an international scene and various cultures across the globe in which religion both figures and is refigured in multiple forms. It finds its way into art, film, advertising, television, popular novels, architecture, video games, popular and classical music, and the manufacture of jewellery. Its predominantly cultural form is manifest in a new investment in mythology. From the Enlightenment up to the third quarter of the twentieth century, myth was regarded as a primitive form of thinking. Its layers were to be peeled back with the tools of reason and empirical analysis. Not now. In big block-buster movies like Christopher's Nolan's *Dark Knight* trilogy (2005–12) and Zack Snyder's *300* (2006), it is not only graphic novels that are making a comeback, but also the mythologies found in them. From Robert Zemeckis' *Beowulf* (2006) and the *Harry Potter* franchise, to the award-winning and phenomenally grossing televised series of George R.R. Martin's *Game of Thrones* novels, myth is once again enchanting us. And religion is always there in the mythic mix. One of the founding fathers of sociology, Max Weber, characterized the cultural conditions emerging from industrialism and instrumental reasoning as 'disenchanted'. But there are any number of social theorists today who want to use the term 're-enchantment' alongside 'post-secularism' to describe our contemporary cultural landscapes. The internet and a laptop make what was once understood as angelic knowledge available to everyone, at least as an idea.

Old mythologies are endlessly revamped, like *Doctor Who*, repackaged for a new market and internationalized. Departments of theology and religion have frequently offered courses in religion and film and theology and literature, examining messianic themes in the movies and religious inspirations in the gothic. There are long-established journals devoted to these studies. But such courses are now being expanded to include, and examine, whole ranges of media and the arts, technological advances, the arcana of theoretical physics and infotainment, to engage with the re-enchanted world as we experience it today.

Millennials were born into a world that is postsecular. That does not mean secularism is over. What it means is that the secular view of the way things are in the world is no longer the predominant one – if, in fact, it ever was. But this has implications – not least for those wishing to study theology and religion and understand the world today. Many of the Millennials are the children of those holding secular views or who did not feel it was right, if they held to a religious faith, to make educating them in that faith a family priority. In the past, this socializing in and through family members, older friends, and peers had played a key role in the transmission of a certain religious tradition over generations. So many of the Millennials grew up not schooled in religious beliefs and practices. Hence the shift in purpose for why we study theology and religion in universities today: the need to provide greater theological literacy so that Millennials might better understand our shared current cultural situation and how we got here. One world-ranking university in the UK, for example, felt it important to employ someone with a background in theology and religion in their English Faculty because they were encountering students who, lacking such theological literacy, were simply unable to understand the language, references, and issues in the work of Shakespeare, the Metaphysical Poets, Milton, or even D.H. Lawrence. They had not read nor had they any acquaintance with the staple literature of earlier generations: the sacred texts – whether that be the Hebrew scriptures, the Christian Bible, the Koran, or the Upanishads.

Theological and religious literacy matters today. We need to know how to read our environment and have a better understanding of where we are. Reading the world well has been the key to our survival from the moment we jumped down from the trees and began to walk upright. It enabled us to flourish with all the new vulnerability that being bi-pedal brought (and all its advantages). We needed to think in order to adapt.

2

Living with Invisibility

Surprisingly, less is said about God or gods than you might think in the study of theology and religion. Little is known. And what is known is known by inference. The walk of faith, whatever the religion, is living with the invisible. So few, if any, would be converted by such a study; and, besides, that it not its purpose. Its purpose is educational: to get at one of the well-springs of civilizations' continual quests to express how the world appears to them, moulding their experiences of what is most valued and what is most significant. These values and significances forever elude us and so forever need to be rearticulated.

So here we are trying to fathom and forage the *Zeitgeist*, the character of our times, using ideas like 'Millennials', 'secularism', 'religion', 'myth', and 'culture' as forensic tools. They are not very precise tools because they are not easy to define and their definitions change over time. We try to hone the edges of these tools and give them more precision through our study and examination of particular articulations of them and what such examinations enable us to understand. Human beings have always done this: tried to make sense of where they are and who they are. The tools have changed and become more sophisticated – from stone axes to the super-proton synchrotron probing the fundamental laws of particle physics. But the goal has remained the same: the human *need* to understand, because understanding has been keyed into our evolution as a basic strategy for surviving as a species. When we ask, then, why the study of theology and religion matters, it matters because what counts as mattering is important to our understanding of the times in which we live. We sift through the overwhelming multiplicity of our experience, individual and collective, and we try to make sense of it. That's what human beings have always done and always will do. And the jury is still out on the extent to which other forms of life, from plants to animals, do the same. Students are attracted to the study of theology and religion because they already appreciate *that* it matters. What drives their intellectual curiosity is *why* it matters.

And at the very epicentre of this inquiry is the word 'God'. It's a word – and that's important to recognize. It's a product of being human. It's not the name of someone or some object 'out there'. Moses, Jesus, Muhammad, are the names of individuals. 'God' is not a word that functions like that, even though, in sacred texts, God or the gods come to the fore as major protagonists in the action of complex plots. That needs thinking about because it has had, has, and will have consequences for what we most value and find most significant. Consequences, that is, for the order of our choices and modes of behavioural response.

In the Book of Genesis, from the Hebrew Scriptures, there's a story about Abraham taking his only son Isaac up Mount Moriah to be offered as a sacrifice. There are certain actors in this story who are represented as human beings with histories and characters (Abraham and Isaac). There is one actor that is an animal (a ram), caught in some brambles, and that replaces Isaac to become the sacrificial victim at the very last moment. There is one character who is definitely not human (the angel of God), who intervenes just as Abraham is about to bring down the knife on his son. And then there is one character (God) who initiates all the action by speaking to Abraham and demanding he make this sacrifice. God doesn't make any physical appearance in the story. God is not represented (though later in the Book of Exodus Moses is given a glimpse of His back parts). God is not representable because God is the author of all that is, and it is only 'all that is' that we can represent in our story-telling about God. So in our very human need to *make* sense, we represent that which is fundamentally unrepresentable. We imagine what is unimaginable. That has had unmissable and unfortunate consequences in the history of the monotheistic faiths (Judaism, Christianity, and Islam). Among other things, it has made God male.

Imagination

A crucial feature of the years of studying theology and religion is coming to terms with what people mean when they speak and write of 'God', 'gods', and the 'divine'. That 'coming to terms' means recognizing that the study of theology and religion is an imaginative science like most of the intellectual disciplines that make up any liberal arts or are housed in a humanities school (literature, history, music, fine art, and so on). Let me explain that before we proceed to examine 'God talk', because

God is subjective

Religion depends on imagination

students studying these disciplines are cultivating and considering critically one of the most powerful human capabilities: the imagination. *as we don't know*

The imagination makes possible _all_ empathy; to appreciate how people of faith think and behave theologically. It is fundamental to any notions of other living beings (human and non-human), community, values, and a sense of belonging. Imagination is prior to and deeper than the ability to reason. As neuroscientists have shown, reasoning operates on the basis of what imagination feeds it, and what reasoning processes is only a tiny fraction of what imagination handles. We imagine continually. Dreaming is the imagination in default mode – consciousness operating at electrical levels beneath wakefulness and when our bodies are rendered inert. Cats and dogs, the animals we know best because we have domesticated them over thousands of years, also dream. So imagination is not just a human capacity. *meta-physical God*

Without an ability to imagine, there would be no study of theology and religion. There would be no religion to study. For, as I said, religious faith is living with the invisible. We live with the invisible more than we often care to think. The air we breathe, the electro-magnetic fields of the earth that have meant we have kept our atmosphere when other planets had it stripped from them, the gravity waves that hold us and the solar system in place – none of these are visible as such. What is visible are the effects of these elements. In a sense, this can also be said of any number of emotions we experience: pain, hope, joy, desire. None of them are visible. *but we know them to exist* Brain scanning and measurements of endocrinal discharges can give us some insight into their activity. But the best insights come from experiencing them and observing other people experiencing them. And, of course, the experiences get translated further into actions, because they affect our behaviour and our moods. I may or may not carry out anything on the basis of my desire, but my doing so or not doing so will each have consequences – psychologically to me and sociologically with respect to other people.

So just because religion walks with the invisible and its study is an imaginative science doesn't make it merely imaginary. The father of psychoanalysis, Sigmund Freud, believed religion dealt with illusions, and eventually we would all come to terms with this and outgrow them.[1] That's not happened to date. Whatever we understand by the word 'God' cannot be made visible (and explicable and

---

[1] Sigmund Freud, *Future of an Illusion*, trans. James Strachey, Penguin Freud Library vol. 12 (London: Penguin Books, 1991).

controllable) in terms of natural forces explored by physics and chemistry or psychological operations explored by cognitive and neuroscientists. But those who practise a religious devotion view the visible effects of the divine everywhere. There is nothing imaginary about the conflicts between Shias and Sunnis in Middle Eastern Islam. There is nothing imaginary about the pogroms and holocausts against Judaism. There is nothing imaginary about the Buddhist violence in Borneo, Sri Lanka, or Myanmar. Genocide has haunted the history of religions because it gets caught up with ethnicity. We'll look at that more closely in the next chapter.

There is nothing imaginary either about the religious conviction and creativity that inspired many of the major cultural artefacts we visit today: the Maya temples, the European cathedrals, the Ottoman mosques, the marble mausoleum of the Taj Mahal, and the Hindu pagodas of Mahabalipuram. And to these architectural marvels we must add the tilework, the statuary, the carvings, the carpets, the vestments, the paintings, the stained glass, ornaments of gold, silver, and bronze, and those gem-studded sacred vessels. Outside of holy sites, only the palaces of sultans, emperors, and kings have received such lavish attention. And these buildings are not just a testimony to the past and a UNESCO heritage. The same religious conviction and creativity is evident today – in completing what remained unfinished (Gaudí's cathedral the Sagrada Familia in Barcelona) and commissioning vast new works (the Temple of Solomon in Bras, downtown São Paulo, Brazil).

Reading

The religious believer negotiates many textures of invisibility, from the natural and cognitive to the spiritual and divine. She draws inferences from the effects of what is unseen, like any of us, reading the world as a sacred text and a sacred text as the world. Let's return briefly to our Neanderthals, because our reading skills began with what is most primitive: tracking a prey for food. We move from a sign to its meaning to enable us to live. If the signs back then were the quality of the wind passing down the valley and the scents it bore or the mud-prints and spores of animals to be hunted, then these were no less signs and meaningful than our alphabetic scripts. They were no less symbolic, though symbolism of another order.

The most complex words the study of theology and religion works with are not 'God' or 'soul'.

They are words we think we understand how to use and that we use all the time: verbs like 'to know' and 'to be', and nouns like 'nature' and 'body'. In Hebrew, there are many different words for 'God'; and in Greek, 'soul' carries a materiality that is finer that the threads of a spider's web: the materiality of breath. There is a link between the Latin for 'soul' (*anima*) and the Greek word for 'wind' (*anemos*), just as there is in the Sanskrit between *atman* (soul) and 'atmosphere'. But 'God' and 'soul' carry with them meanings of hiddenness and mystery because of their long association with the invisible, whereas 'to know', 'to be', 'nature', and 'body' seem to lack a density of meaning. I know of few better ways of retrieving and appreciating the density in those words (and others we use with such familiarity) than learning to read the languages of the ancients, and how those languages express the beliefs and sacred values of the peoples who spoke and, eventually, wrote them.

There's only room for one example.

I have not learnt Sanskrit, pitifully, but when I read in a translation of Psalm 23 'he maketh me to lie down in green pastures; he leadeth me by the still waters' I am in an English meadow in springtime. I'm citing the King James Version here, which Shakespeare himself may have had a hand in translating or advising the translators. I'm employing it because the old-fashioned terms of 'maketh' and 'leadeth' that give us some poetic distance and help make the text a little less familiar. The Psalm opens, famously, with 'the Lord is my shepherd', but the Hebrew of what is now verse 2 begins with the waters not the pastures for sheep. Only the consonants were provided in the ancient text; a reader acquainted with the oral tradition supplied the vowels. When the text was transcribed and disseminated by the Masoretes (a group of Rabbinic Jews) somewhere between the seventh and the tenth centuries CE, the vowels provided emphasized the liquid character of the Hebrew. The repeated consonants are soft *waw*s, *lamed*s, *mem*s, and *nun*s (w's, l's, m's, and n's), giving the expression an alliteration that hushes and soothes. And to these sounds are added open vowels giving expression to assonance and internal rhyming that quells and quiets. The water described isn't flowing; the movement comes from the one (the Lord) who is leading me (the first person who describes a movement that is close to floating). This is not a Scottish burn or an English brook. It is not a river at all. It's an oasis where the waters stretch out beneath the sun, unruffled by the wind. Behind this depiction lie mile after mile of desert sand and wind-carved wadis, and a nomadic Bronze Age existence between far-flung mud-baked cities in a harsh terrain.

But there is something more here also: a deep memory of an association between land and language. The Psalm was sung, verbalized, and recited for thousands of years before it was written down. The oral nature of speech mimics natural sounds. When I hear Xhosa spoken in South Africa today – only written down by white men in the nineteenth century – the various clicks, whistles, and clucks combine with breathing and flows of sounds taken directly from the natural world in which the African people found themselves. For these hunters, speech was a means of communicating in a landscape without being detected; a way of becoming animals among all the other animals. So, in this Psalm, the Hebrew letter *lamed* is the word for a shepherd's staff (to defend the sheep) and is written like a crooked rod; *mem* is the word for river and is written like a wave; and *nun* is related to the word for fish. Letters *live* in Hebrew; they have animated power. Even abstract words like 'force' and 'glory' are inseparable from material forms like 'arm' and 'weight'. Later, in Jewish Kabbalistic mysticism, letters had the power to conjure because of their profound kinship with cosmic elements and spirits. Creation was conceived as a literary composition by

God using Hebrew letters. Here, in this Psalm, the very consonants of the language enact their early pictographic form in which the sound related to the natural world. As we listen to it, and shape the words with our own mouths, we recover something of the oral tradition beneath later literacy, and the felt two-way relationship between language and land.

To read the sacred text in the ancient language is to enter the poetry of another civilization where the key relationship is between a people and their environment; a people who have survived and can continue to survive because they have learnt to read the land, its weather, its potential for food and, most particularly, water. To read is to encounter the one who goes before to protect and provide – *El-Shaddai*, the liberal and benevolent Lord. It is to encounter 'nature' as something lived, participated in, and deeply interwoven with a sense of a people's utter dependence on what it gives and takes. We find a people in this text totally exposed and profoundly in communication with rock, earth, sky, water, grass, and the animals that feed upon it.

You can't get that from the English translation. The West is awash and wasteful when it comes to water. It has forgotten how vital it is to life. 'Still' or 'quiet' water allows all the sediment to sink. It becomes jewel-like beneath a vast blue awning, clear and cool. A whole ecology is summed up in that one verse, ordered, invisibly, by the one who created and sustains it. However 'God' is understood here (the word 'Yahweh' is used, a word full of air and breath), this deity is not some super-authoritarian figure. He or She or It is radically associated with all that is the land – the people's relationship to it and dependence upon it.

God Talk

What this engagement with a sacred Hebrew text reveals – and reveals about all sacred texts, whatever the religion they are associated with – is that talk about God or the divine, however transcendent and exalted that God or divinity is, can never be separated from language used in everyday life. Whenever people of faith say 'God speaks', it's a metaphor. Famously, Mother Teresa, when interviewed about her prayer life, was asked what God said to her. 'He doesn't,' she replied. 'He listens.' It was God's silence that 'spoke'. We'll come back to silence later.

Sacred texts, like theological texts more generally, are products of human culture. That is, human beings living in human communities in specific times and places employ human languages to compose them. This becomes particularly important in faith traditions founded upon a notion of direct communication between the divine and the human, and where the sacred text has been viewed as revealed truth. In these traditions, some would understand the Bible or the Koran as 'infallible' access to truth that cannot be questioned The text, though it has to be read, does not need to be interpreted. This is difficult and potentially very dangerous, both psychologically and politically. Because the idea that a text, down to its vowel sounds and punctuation, is dictated by God goes well beyond a text being divinely inspired. It encourages the idea that the text has the power to speak for itself – even though it has to be read if it is be engaged with at all.

I well remember, following a lecture I gave on the Christian theologian John Calvin, a man rising angrily from the back of the auditorium. He shook his Bible and shouted: 'This is the Word of God. It speaks clearly. It doesn't need interpreting.' I probably didn't help the situation by telling him he was holding a translation; and a translation *is* an interpretation. All reading is an interpretation. No written text speaks in this literal fashion; linguistic symbols have to be decoded. There have been cultures wary of writing things down, and cultures in which sacred texts could only be handled by those selected or ordained to do so. But that puts a great deal of power and authority in the hands of those who can write and those who are allowed to read. When that power and authority is given divine sanction and faithful adherents are given no critical distance from what is so written or read, then priestly regimes are open to the abuse of power and individuals to self-delusion.

And indeed, in the Reformed tradition of the seventeenth century, there were theologians claiming that God dictated every word (Hebrew or Greek) and the authors of the Christian Scriptures simply took it down. The seventeenth-century English writer John Bunyan (author of *The Pilgrim's Progress*) wrote one of the earliest modern autobiographies, *Grace Abounding to the Chief of Sinners* (1666), dedicated to his conversion to Christianity. Though printed books (and Bibles) had been available for over a century and a half, Bunyan belonged to a rural community that was still very much rooted in an oral culture. When he read the Bible, he heard it speaking to him; God speaking to him and, more particularly, Satan speaking to him. Battles reigned in his head and ears, holy wars between the voice of God and the voice of Satan, until he was literally running down the country lanes away from their clamorous demands. It reached a point where, though he was fond of bell ringing, he couldn't bear to stand beneath a church tower (a 'steeplehouse'):

> I began to think, how, if one of the bells should fall? Then I chose to stand under a main beam that lay overthwart the steeple from side to side, thinking there I might stand sure: but then I should think again, should the bell fall with a swing, it might first hit the wall, and then rebounding upon me, might kill me for all this beam; this made me stand in the steeple door; and now, thought I, I am safe enough, for if a bell should then fall, I can slip out behind these thick walls, and so be preserved notwithstanding.
>
> So, after this, I would yet go to see them ring, but would not go further than the steeple door; but then it came into my head, how if the steeple itself should fall? And this thought, (it may fall for ought I know) would when I stood and looked on, continually so shake my mind, that I durst not stand at the steeple door any longer, but was forced to flee, for fear the steeple should fall upon my head.[2]

On the edge of a nervous breakdown and prey to bouts of terrifying paranoia, Bunyan came to

[2] John Bunyan, *Grace Abounding to the Chief of Sinners*, ed. W.R. Owens (Harmondsworth: Penguin Books, 1987), pp. 13–14.

his senses when he recognized the Bible was to be read and, in being read, interpreted. It didn't speak directly with either the voice of God or the voice of Satan. It could not speak a single word of itself.

Interpretation

God's own relation to 'God talk' (and even a sacred text is a form of 'God talk') is speculative. Whatever may have been the 'conversation' between Abraham and Yahweh recorded in the Book of Genesis, the form in which we have received knowledge of that 'conversation' is a written narrative authored in a particular language in a particular place by a human being. Whatever the parables as 'spoken' in, presumably, Aramaic by Jesus Christ, we have received them through some writer or writers who composed them for us in *koine* Greek. And you can do things in ancient Hebrew you can't do in Greek (like conflate the present with the future tense) – and vice versa.

For this reason, ancient scribes and sages proposed certain general rules to govern the interpretation of sacred texts; rules that could be taught, that could be passed down, and that drew attention to the writing and the reading of the text. If the Sanskrit

Sutras attended more to rules about living and behaving well, rather than how to interpret texts, in the Jewish tradition there were two sets of rules for interpreting the Torah, by two different rabbis, teaching in the second century BCE: the seven rules of Rabbi Hilliel and the thirteen rules of Rabbi Ishmael. As the Scriptural canon was formed in the Christian tradition, so discussion began about how to interpret that text (and its relation to the Hebrew Scriptures). Famously, St Augustine devoted a whole book to this task, *On Christian Teaching*,[3] and a highly complex four-fold method of 'exegesis' (which is what interpretation was called) was developed by scholars from late antiquity to mediaeval times. The Koran, too, has developed rules for its exegesis to help safeguard against interpretations that are not in line with Islamic law. There is a recognition here of the power and authority of sacred texts, how they might be abused, and how there is a need to learn *how* to read these texts well. World history is strewn with religious causes won or lost on the grounds of interpretation and the bad reading of texts.

[3] St Augustine, *On Christian Teaching*, trans. R.P.H. Green (Oxford: Oxford University Press, 1997).

The Sacred Ways of Saying

All this reading and interpreting of a literary production raises the question of what we mean then by 'sacred' when we refer to such a text. If the divine is conceived as the uncreated creator, 'that than which nothing greater can be conceived' (to quote the twelfth-century saint Anselm), then the use of human language to depict the nature and activity of the divine is attempting the impossible. It is trying to talk of what is unimaginable, beyond language, and outside all created comprehension. So we find certain rhetorical strategies are employed to push human expression towards the inexpressible.

There's exaggerated language for example, which piles up excessive titles. A Hindu prayer to Lord Shiva describes him as 'the Master of the universe, the great Lord . . . the glorious God of Gods'. There are comparisons or analogies between the familiar and what is radically outside ordinary human experience and unfamiliar. This can give rise to anthropomorphisms, where human characteristics and behaviours are attributed to the actions of the divine or spiritual affects: God is angry or even God is loving. Metaphors can be used in which traits from one object or act are transferred in a description of quite a different object or act. Some attributes of the divine in monotheism employ a negative suffix. 'Infinite', for example, comes from the Latin *fines* meaning 'boundary', but by putting the Latin *in* as a suffix the words comes to mean 'without boundaries' or 'beyond all boundaries'. Another such negation is 'ineffable' – where effability is the capacity to express or describe something in words. 'Ineffable' means 'beyond expression' or the ability to describe in words. Mystical writers of all traditions wishing to describe and communicate something of their experience of encountering the divine will often use such forms of negation, the most extreme of which is the paradox or oxymoron like 'darkness visible.'

Islam is rich in mystical poetry. This is taken from an example of such verse composed by the ninth-century Persian teacher of Sufism, Mansur al-Hallaj. Many of the rhetorical uses of language I have outlined above are evident in its expression (and translation into English):

I asked, 'Who are You?' He answered, 'You!'
For You one cannot ask, Where?
Because where is Where for You?

You do not pass through the imagination
Or else we'll know where You are.

You are He who is everywhere
Yet nowhere. Where are You?

In my relinquishment is my relinquishment's
   relinquishment
And You are there in my relinquishment.[4]

The concluding lines of the poem point to a familiar resort of those who wish to speak of God – silence. The Arabic for 'relinquishment' is *fanā*, which means 'passing away' (like a breath of wind). It's a gentle word of release – though the standard translation of the poem uses 'annihilation'. *Fanā* expresses a profound letting-go to the point and place where words come to an end and the invisible enfolds all things. *Fanā* is the final step in the Sufi's mystic journey.

The practice of silence, and meditation within and upon silence, is a common feature of devotion in all the major faith traditions. In the Christian tradition, St Augustine writes of the silences that are between words like the intervals between musical notes, and it is in the silences where the presence of God is found. And in the Jewish tradition there is

---

[4] Mansur al-Hallaj, 'I witnessed my Creator with my heart's eye' is available online: *http://www.poetry-chaikhana.com/blog/2011/11/07/mansur-al-hallaj-i-witnessed-my-maker/*. I have adapted a translation by Mahmood Jamal from the Arabic.

the famous story of the prophet Elijah. Persecuted by King Ahab and his wife Jezebel, he challenged the prophets of Baal to a competition in which the Lord God came down with lightning to ignite a water-drenched pyre. Knowing the murderous intentions of the king and his wife, he flees and then the Lord tells him to stand on the mountain of Horeb, 'for the Lord is about to pass by.' Elijah obeys and

> Then a great and powerful wind tore the mountains apart and shattered the rocks before the Lord, but the Lord was not in the wind. After the wind there was an earthquake, but the Lord was not in the earthquake. After the earthquake came a fire, but the Lord was not in the fire. And after the fire came a gentle whisper. When Elijah heard it, he pulled his cloak over his face and went out and stood at the mouth of the cave. (1 Kings 19:11–13)

The Hebrew for that 'gentle whisper' is more literally the paradox 'the voice of gentle silence'. It's a word resonant with 'm' sounds – like the Tibetan mantra 'Om', known in Hinduism, Buddhism, Jainism, and Sikhism.

You can't do very much investigative work with silence, but its treatment as the ground-base of the life and experience of worship in many of the world faiths is the condition from which cultic practices emerge and to which they return. It brings to the fore a demand in the study of theology and religion for continual awareness that whatever the intellectual analysis pursued at a distance in the classroom, piety for religious believers is a way of living and experiencing and making sense of life. So there are new trends in the way faith traditions are being looked at and examined. Cross-disciplinary work is necessary to do this work. It might mean coming alongside anthropologists attending to ethnographies of liturgy and ritual based on conversations with worshippers and first-hand accounts. It might mean working with sociologists exploring how what are called 'emotional communities' formed; communities where certain emotions are valued and cultivated (love, mercy, joy) and others are excluded (hate, anger, fear). It might mean working with cognitive scientists investigating 'priming', where attitudes and moods are invoked by the very physical nature of posture: eyes lifted, kneeling, standing and facing east, bowing, for example.

All these cross-disciplinary studies are employed to understand religious belief and religious conviction at a time when we witness them as the driving motivations for acts of unthinkable violence or acts of self-sacrificial caring. And that understanding is essential because it is experience of the divine that fills the naming and the figuring of God or gods with content. The study of theology and religion cannot ignore the extraordinary power of such experiences.

I was once working with a small class of various religious believers and non-believers on a text by the French philosopher Michel de Certeau on what makes a belief believable. As we discussed the different types of believing, one in the group asked, 'Why do people believe?' The question wasn't aimed at anyone in particular. It arose directly from the essay we were studying. But it became an important classroom moment because it was followed by a more personal address to a member of the group who was wearing a Sikh turban. 'Why do you believe?' The Sikh was a mature student and not at all fazed by the question. He thought for a moment and began by saying his family came from Pakistan. I suppose we all thought he was going to tell us something about the way he had been brought up. But he began to speak briefly about how his life and his parents' lives had not been at all easy. There had been some ups and a lot of downs. And then he concluded simply with his answer to the question: 'It works.' And somehow that released some others in the group who also were believers – Quakers and Christians mainly[5] – to agree. It was a Jewish person who spoke last, reminding the group of a Psalm in which the writer spoke of times of affliction and times of benefaction, but through it all God had been faithful.

For me it was a rare moment, neither sought for nor orchestrated, where something between faith traditions became apparent, though I couldn't say what. There was a time when some philosophers of religion wrote about all religions being rooted in the same Ultimate Reality that simply took on local colouring, names, and symbols. But that is not what was being affirmed in that class. And from what exalted state can anyone, philosopher or otherwise, make a claim about Ultimate Reality? What 'God' names, what 'divine' signifies, are not the same in Judaism, Christianity, Hinduism, Sikhism, Buddhism, and Islam. The very meaning and feel of the words change with the language used, the variety of traditions (even within one religious faith), and the ways in which religious believing (and conviction) operates at levels of physiology as well as psychology. Words like 'God' and 'divine' come to mean what they mean not just through teaching and

---

[5] Not all Quakers identify as Christian, and there is considerable debate about the overlap and difference.

social/cultural formation. They are meaningful also because of life experiences.

The study of theology and religion assists in developing a deeper appreciation of religious experiences in a world that is shared, and in which our survival as a species depends upon the manner in which that sharing takes place.

3

Religion and Power

This is not a good story. Religion is powerful – coercively so. Religion is also empowering, generating solidarity, inspiring hope, and developing aspirations for better ways of living and acting. Like love, and often in the name of love, it can provide both what is most beautiful and what is most imprisoning. But either way, the positive use and the negative abuse of religious power can never be erased from our histories. Its power, though, can be better understood, and that is what the study of theology and religion attempts to provide. Whatever the ambitions of secularism, religion can never be divorced from politics.

A sacred text cannot exist in splendid isolation on scrolls and codices. It's found in libraries, composed in mediaeval monastic writing rooms, or *scriptoria*, preserved in archives or richly decorated caskets, and housed in dedicated spaces. A sacred text, because it is sacred, gathers about itself social institutions, staffed by trained acolytes and servants. And down the back corridors of any one of these institutions, questions of authority and power resound. Why was this one Neanderthal man found buried, his skeleton intact, at the heart of the Shanidar cave deep in the Zagros Mountains? As I said in the Introduction, there were other burials in the same place, but this man's body is buried very carefully, centrally, and in a foetal position. Some people are treated as more valuable than other people, particularly those invested with, or seen to possess, distinctive gifts. Gifts of healing, leadership, and control over the elements set them aside from the ordinary and situate them in a limbo between worlds that are seen and worlds that are unseen.

Texts have to be produced and, as we have seen, read. Reading, too, is part of a social institution that emerges in oral cultures and constitutes social memories. If the first forms of writing seem to be records of business transactions, religious groups discovered the power of scripted communication early and put it to good and bad use. In some cultures, both learning to write and learning to read were restricted to certain elites, as access to education was also restricted. Even in oral cultures, however, the languages spoken can be bearers of social value distinguishing native from foreigner, the civilized from the barbarian, the labourer from the aristocrat. Class distinctions and hierarchy are as old as religion and frequently model themselves on it.

There has never been a religion that is not political. Even the counter-cultural Amish (a Christian church of Swiss Anabaptist origins) who live in remote and isolated communities separated from others and holding to their own traditions of dress, housing, transport, and cuisine make a political statement. As do the Druze on the Israeli–Lebanese border, the Hasidic Jews in their Jerusalem enclave, the Cham Muslims in Vietnam and Cambodia. Here religion cannot be divorced from race and ethnicity, however much these groups refuse to participate in the machinery of state governance. Their counter-cultural stance is an act of political, social, and cultural resistance.

So the relationship between religion and politics should come as no surprise. In the wake of global history since at least the rise of the Muslim Brotherhood in Egypt in the 1920s (and the politicization of Islam) and following the fall of the Shah of Iran in the late 1970s, increasing attention has been paid to that relationship in the study of theology and religion. It would not be unusual to find courses examining 'political theology' or 'political religion' in the university. Both terms have an intellectual provenance that goes right back to the Roman scholar Marcus Terentius Varro (116–27 BCE) in the West.

Law and Legitimation

The question governing the relationship between religion and politics is the recognized authority that justifies the exercise of power. Power is never anonymous. Individuals or groups of individuals wield it. Authority to exercise power is either bestowed by the people being ruled or seized by one means or another. In an elected government, the power is bestowed by the electorate (often, and misguidedly, understood as 'the people'). They consent to be ruled through representatives voted for democratically. The democratic system authorizes them to exercise power. In a dictatorship, power is seized by an individual backed by groups of elites (like the military). The people need not consent. Might, in whatever form, enforces rule. The exercise of power is not authorized so much as imposed. In an oligarchy, the power is shared by a selected or self-appointed number of elites acting on behalf of the political order or state. Power is exercised on behalf of a people who consent to be ruled by these chosen ones.

Religion need not play any direct role in any of these forms of government, though, indirectly, it can support them or deny them support, as we shall see. In a theocracy (where religion and politics are most closely allied), the deity itself authorizes the exercise of power over the people through recognized ministers of that deity. The right to exercise power can be given directly by God, with the king or pharaoh or emperor as the 'son' of God and himself divine. Or the divine right to exercise power can be given indirectly, with the monarch as the 'representative' of God on earth and divinely appointed to rule. In Europe, following those Wars of Religion I spoke of in Chapter 1, a number of national monarchs (kings like Louis XIV of France or Charles II of England) claimed their sovereignty was based on 'divine right'. Tsars in Russia and kings in Prussia made a similar claim. There was a tension in this 'divine right' – for the sovereign was both the one who ruled and the one beyond that rule. As law-maker and law-enforcer, his power (usually it was a 'he') was transcendent and exceptional. But the question governing the exercise of power, and the divine authority bestowed, concerns not just its source but also its legitimacy: that is, the recognition by the ruled that the power of the ruler is 'rightful'. The sovereign one must show his god-like power. French and English monarchs, for example, were believed to have the 'royal touch' that could cure diseases.

It was by a demonstration of god-like power that a rule was legitimated as divine. If the power of the shaman did not bring healing, did not ward off the evil spirits, did not help the hunt and protect the crops, did not assist in the bringing of rain, the aversion of disaster, and the appeasement of the anger of the gods, then that shaman's power was questionable and his legitimacy *as* a shaman was doubted. In the realm of religious politics, whether as a tsar or an emperor, results count if the exercise of power is to be recognized as rightful.

At stake is the meaningfulness of life itself: either what happens in life is arbitrary and fundamentally anarchic (so we need someone who can hold back the deluge and keep wolverine human beings from destroying each other) or there is a 'cosmos' (which the Greeks understood as an ordering of things). Religion may walk with the invisible and believe in what is unseen, but its essential intuition is that life is meaningful; that there is an order and an ordering of things in and through the divine act of creating the world. That meaning may not be clearly comprehensible – after all, we are not its creators, only part of its created orders – but if 'Things fall apart' and 'the centre cannot hold' (as the Irish poet W.B. Yeats wrote in 'The Second Coming'), then 'Mere anarchy is loosed upon the world.' The religious authority to exercise power is based upon a meaningful and ordered world, and if the ruler cannot maintain this order (and its meaningfulness), then the rule is not rightful: he (and occasionally she) is not the chosen one.

Seeking Justice

Organized religions proclaim and teach that there is a 'way' to live in accordance with this divine ordering of things, and that right living is rewarded with divine blessings In Hebrew this is *Derek* – a word closely associated with justice. When we think of justice today in the US we think of a woman seated in judgement outside the Supreme Court in Washington. It's a statue in marble by James Earle Fraser. She rests one arm on a book and in the other she holds a smaller statue of herself as blindfolded, a set of scales held tightly in her arms. Similar scales are held in the left hand of lady justice carved in bas-relief on the lampposts at the front of the building. In these depictions she clutches the sword in her right hand, its point resting on the ground.

This is an ancient symbol. Maybe the woman represents the protective mother, sheltering everyone without prejudice, under her caring sway. Maybe she is a symbol of virgin innocence, beyond the pollutions of competing human interests. Either way, modern secular notions of justice are founded today upon human rights, enshrined in certain constitutions: in America, first (1787), then France (1791), and now in many other countries. One of the most comprehensive constitutions enshrining human rights is the South African one, ratified when apartheid came to an end in 1994. But human rights are very difficult to implement; they are continually and even openly violated. Human rights embrace the whole species of humankind. They proclaim that we are one kind. And that means that while one suffers, we all suffer. While one person is persecuted, we are all vulnerable to persecution. While one person's freedom is curtailed, then none of us are as free as we would like to believe. Human rights long for and aspire towards justice, but human beings are continually unable to live up to them; so we growl like bears.

There are endless debates among political theorists as to what grounds this modern, secular understanding of justice. What relates human rights to a meaningful order of things rather than being simply pragmatic? What is the transcending condition that makes them universally applicable? Is it a 'common sense' of what is the right way to behave towards each other? Is it an agreed contract that recognizes that human beings left to their own whims and desires would tear each other apart, and so there needs to be a shared agreement consenting to the governing rules of a nation state? Is it the law of nature such that human beings are made in a certain way with certain natural and social affections and responsibilities? How do we live together peacefully and flourish, as individuals and communities? Is there any approved consensus at to what that peaceable living and flourish looks like? How do we govern ourselves?

Human rights constitute a good benchmark. They are often viewed as independent of religion, though the ethical teaching in the traditional world faiths not only subscribes to, but also promotes them. Some would argue that such rights have their inspiration and origin in a religious appreciation for the dignity of the human beings as created by God. But would we all agree on what these rights should be? The right to work, for example, puts a marker in the sand. To work is to contribute and is often recognized as an important part of self-affirmation and a sense of dignity. But, given the unpredictable nature of economic climates, what nation state can guarantee a 'right' to work? And some forms of work are dehumanizing and exploitative. Should there be a 'right' to clean water? After all, water is the most basic need of all human beings. But water is plentiful in some parts of the world and scarce in others – like oil, or minerals, or gemstones. Because of our dependence upon it and the unequal nature of its distribution, it becomes recognized as a 'resource' to be managed. As a 'resource', it becomes a commodity. Not one human being can do without water. Nevertheless, it is more available to some than others, and as a commodity it can be bought, sold, provided, or withdrawn.

Human rights are a good benchmark, as I said, but they remain human, and in the hands of humans. And as our histories towards each other demonstrate, our dispositions as humans are not always kindly. We are, after all, animals with advanced cognitive powers. We are here because we survived while other species became extinct. And they became extinct not simply due to climate change: often humans hunted them to extinction. Moreover, humans continually direct this destructive violence against each other: war and genocide disfigure our histories as a species, and have raised over centuries of reflection the question of evil.

Evil

At some point in the study of theology and religion, 'evil' will be encountered (often prefaced with 'the problem of'). It might be in a course on the philosophy of religion, where evil is examined with respect to the omnipotence of God and what is called 'theodicy'. Questions are raised here like: if God is omnipotent, why is evil permitted? Or what account of God's dealings with creation can we give that enables us to understand the atrocities that all too frequently beset us – from natural disasters to the systematic extermination of one class of people by another? Is God good but fallible? Or is God infallible but not good? Are there two or more competing sovereign powers, on one side for good and on the other for evil, and all things created are caught up in a cosmic theatre of war in which, inevitably, there is going to be some collateral damage? Are there two sides to the one supreme deity – a face of wrath and a face of benevolence – subject to divine whim?

The question of evil might be encountered in courses on religious ethics. Here the stakes are high, but it is not necessarily the nature of the divine that is being cross-examined. What is of more concern in religious ethics is how far humans are responsible and how we should act in accordance with divine ordinances (the law of God). The focus is moral evil: how we act towards one another. But here's the rub: divine ordinances are extracted from sacred texts, written in ancient times, for ancient situations, and in ancient languages. How we act towards one another today is governed by civil law, liberal notions of maximizing equality, respect for others, toleration and, as I said, human rights. Here the sacred and the secular can collide head on, sometimes violently, in issues on abortion, sexual orientation and practice, gay marriage, and ecology. Furthermore, here the sacred encounters issues not even conceived of in the holy books: the use of stem cells, gene therapies, assisted reproduction (IVF), drone warfare, and the ethics of AI (among others). And, as I pointed out in the previous chapter, there is no easy way of extracting rules for conduct from ancient books for contemporary application.

The question of evil will also be at the forefront of theological teachings themselves. For all faiths reflect upon a human condition subject to outward oppressions and inward dispositions to wickedness in their various manifestations. The way of justice

(*Derek*) is the way of righteousness, walking in an upright manner. But this is contrasted to the violences of unrighteousness, sin, transgression, and disobedience. Key to understanding these violences, in both Christianity and Islam, is the notion of original sin: that is, a fundamental rupture in the relationship between God and human beings that came about through human self-assertion. Judaism does not have this notion, though its theological concepts of 'salvation' and 'redemption' are concerned with a reconciliation between the divine and human, and the founding of social life based on that reconciliation. This salvation, and the new right relations it establishes between all that is created, is generally understood as a deliverance from evil. And the power that brings about this deliverance? Is it divine only, or the divine in co-operation with humankind? Who brings about this deliverance, this liberation, this sacred order on earth?

We return again to the association of religion and power.

Demanding Justice

The black Christian theologian Martin Luther King, Jr, once said: 'Power without love is reckless and abusive and love without power is sentimental and anaemic. Power at its best is love implementing the demands of justice. Justice at its best is love correcting everything that stands against love.'[1] He was writing at a time (the late 1960s) when the 'rights of man' were undergoing something of an upheaval as the world woke up to the fact that several groups of people were being systematically excluded from these rights: Asians, Latinos and Latinas, Blacks, gays, women, principally. Attention to class oppression and poverty had arisen in the wake of the Industrial Revolution in the West and the polemics of Karl Marx and Friedrich Engels, but to this were now added the oppressions of gender, race, and ethnicity. A scramble of identity politics with calls for radical transformation or revolution ensued. Colonialism was on its knees, democracy was floundering, and the Cold War was experiencing record-breaking glacial temperatures. From the 1960s and on into the present century, the world order has been changing dramatically – and behind many of those changes, whether in Washington, Tehran, Java, San Salvador, or London, are the

---

[1] The full text of the 1967 speech from which this is taken, 'Where Do We Go From Here?', is available at: *https://kinginstitute.stanford. edu/king-papers/documents/where-do-we-go-here-address-delivered-eleventh-annual-sclc-convention.*

reading, interpretation, and inspiration of sacred texts. Theology inhaled the heady scents of liberation, revolution, and conservative reaction – from the Ayatollah Khomeini's fatwas (religious rulings) to President Reagan's Bible studies in the Oval Office; from the radicalization of Hindus in India to an Israeli Ambassador at a meeting of the UN Security Council clutching the Hebrew Scriptures and claiming the land was theirs; from the call to follow Jesus the liberator in Latin America to the ethnic violence of Theravada Buddhism in Thailand and Sri Lanka. From the beginning of this present century, a 'clash of civilizations' was openly debated.[2]

Meanwhile, a new international order was emerging that was less political and more economic: global free-trade capitalism – though that, too, may be morphing at present. It's an order challenging the old sovereignty of the nation state because all nations are caught up with networks of commodity exchange. And there are some new players: China, Russia, India, for example. In many ways, it's more hostile to religious devotion than secularism is; and perhaps more exploitative than colonialism.

[2] Inspired by Samuel P. Huntington, *The Clash of Civilizations and the Remaking of World Order* (New York: Simon & Schuster, 1996).

It is hostile on two fundamental counts. First, wealth generation from unconstrained capitalism is indifferent to people. When neo-liberal economics, in which the market is sovereign, was initially advocated, there was a belief that lower taxes, giving more freedom to how people wished to spend (or save) their money, would have a 'trickle-down' effect. The more wealth created, then the more jobs there would be, and people's livelihoods would, overall, improve. That has proved a myth: the rich have exponentially increased their wealth and the number now listed among the poor has similarly increased. Power here, economic power, isn't being distributed; it's being centralized. Economic freedom is freedom for those who can afford to be free; the rest are enslaved. And no appeal to justice can be made when money is sovereign – because in itself money is indifferent. So financial power may be global in reach and transcending all boundaries (increasingly as money is digitalized) – it has, in this, divine qualities – but it is unconcerned about justice, the cultivation of relations in which all things are reconciled, or an ecological caring for creation.

Secondly, all religious faiths have a social ethics because they see community as highly valuable for human flourishing. The poor, the widow, the orphaned, and the refugee are the focus for teachings regarding almsgiving, loan-making, a just wage, and friendship. The cultivation of compassion and kinship and rules for simple living form their followers in daily, spiritual practices. Devout Muslims offer a prayer over food that is wasted and needs to be thrown away. These acts, values, and spiritualities are part of the redemption sought for all. Hospitality and generosity are treated as sacred; selfishness, dishonest dealing, and deception are criticized. The economy is there for human exchange, even enterprise, but it can never be sovereign for those of religious faith. The economy serves human beings; they and their energies are not there to provide its battery power like the characters in the movie *The Matrix* (1999).

Because of this friction between religious convictions and the current world order, different faiths have, in their different ways, demanded justice. In doing so, they appeal to a higher sovereignty passed down through the stories, teachings, and practices of their traditions: a divine justice upheld by a divine power working to establish right relations. And on earth that means a participation for all peoples in both political and economic forms of power – that these material forces might better serve them. After all, even Martin Luther King's 'love' has to work through material circumstances and social relations

– otherwise it means nothing to us and can have no effect upon us. But that demand for holy justice can generate frictions of its own.

Beijing, 2005

It might have been a Bond movie.

I'm seated in the office of the Minister of Foreign Affairs, in a low building modelled on Chinese imperial architecture for palaces and temples. (Religious matters in China come under 'foreign affairs'.) The minister is leaner and younger than I expected, and dressed immaculately in a blue tailored suit, white shirt, and tie. The fan overhead is turning slowly, though the temperature of the room is a controlled warm. He smiles across his desk at me, revealing impeccably white teeth, and our interview begins: 'How do you like China, Professor?' The question is delivered in neutral, courteous tones, but his face is a mask, and his eyes stare right into me, scanning my face for flickers of emotion that might express themselves as flushes or muscular tics. This is a test.

I was to be in Beijing for five days with all expenses paid by the Chinese government. I had been put up at a hotel next to the Forbidden City, was driven everywhere in a black limo by my own driver, and was accompanied by a translator who also served in the ministry. The ministry official waited for me in the lobby of the hotel whenever I went up to my room. He watched me ascend in the lift at the end of the day and he greeted me with a smile whenever I came down in the morning. Everything about my visit was planned and organized. There would even be one occasion, an evening when the Beijing fog was thick and I was being hosted at a restaurant, when I was escorted through the city, back and front, by military police.

For a good while the minister and I exchange opinions in a way that gives each of us the impression we are relaxed. Then abruptly the first real question is slipped into the conversation. 'What is your opinion of human rights, Professor?' The conversation takes a more serious turn. He is fishing, weighing, assessing. We toss back and forth various East/West issues. Then we arrive at the point of my visit. 'We have some difficulties understanding the Christian faith as it is practised here in China,' he says, or something quite close to it. 'We have no difficulties with the Christian faith as such,' he adds, quickly. 'But it doesn't seem Chinese in the way it's practised. We wonder if you might be able to assist us.'

Up until that point I had never been to a Christian

service in China, though I had read the biographies of missionaries and stories of persecution were commonplace. Now I was being asked to visit various churches and theological colleges where future Christian ministers were being trained, and meet over lunch and dinner several leaders from different Christian denominations in China. Back in his office, I am assuming the minister is referring to the astonishing growth in Christian fundamentalism. I had heard this was taking place throughout mainland China as the country opened itself more to the Pacific Rim. But he doesn't refer to fundamentalism, at least not directly. Choosing his words with exceptional care, he informs me, 'We would like an indigenous Chinese Christianity. A state church, perhaps, along the lines of your own Church of England.' The 'difficulty' he was referring to is an 'Americanized' Christianity heavily sponsored by US dollars.

Since then I have been in similar situations: in Delhi, where India hosted an international meeting to go through the new constitution of Egypt with Egyptian diplomats following the revolution of the Arab Spring; in Ukraine with leaders of the ecumenical council of churches discussing the role of traditional religion in the new constitution with a government official who was involved in drafting it;

in Singapore, before the Minister of Culture, advising on multi-faith relations in a pluralist secular state threatened with waves of xenophobia against Muslims arising from the success of American-sponsored conservative evangelicalism.

In all these situations, religion was at the forefront of discussions. In China, it was a matter of ensuring a distinctive national identity. With Egypt, we were examining how the coming together of Islamic law (Sharia) and constitutional law affected human rights. In Ukraine, the conversations focused on safeguarding the nation's Eastern Orthodox tradition. And in Singapore, the state was seeking advice on how it could best curb conflicts arising between different religious faiths.

The Challenge

Radicalization, like fundamentalism, is not confined to Islam – though there are strong missionizing, that is, colonizing, drives in both Islam and Christianity. And, on the basis of history and tradition, some religious faiths have strong territorial holds they seek to maintain (and expand) by the oppression or expulsion of minorities or 'aliens'. The new international order is fragile, and insecurities incubate xenophobias. The waves of economic refugees, climate refugees, and asylum seekers will inevitably continue. The dwindling of earth's resources, swelling populations, and ecological changes will provoke power-grabs and enforce exiles. The question is an ancient one, but with no obvious contemporary solution: how do we live together and govern ourselves at national and international levels? We are no longer talking about Greek or Italian city-states and no longer are homogeneous nations made up of those people, generations deep, who have lived and worked there. We are talking about globalized, multi-faith situations in which power and politics can no longer be contained by secular, bureaucratic ideals. Religions will play their part, a major part, in any future clash of ideologies, because they, too, are power-players and religions can, all too easily, become ideological. Religion cannot be and will not be divested of its political power. But religious power is not necessarily at the level of faith-based institutions. Its real power lies at the level of the imagination, with the conviction and aspiration it can mobilize. It is not at all clear what part religions might play in any future reconciliations, though they hold profound creative resources for peace, healing, and hospitality in their teachings, in their texts, and in their rituals.

The study of theology and religion will not provide a solution. After all, however much access is widened for education at university level, and rightly so, universities will educate the elites or those aspiring to become elites. An education in theology and religion has to move out beyond universities and enter social policy if we, as a human species, are to learn to respect and understand; learning to challenge and critique in informed ways, what various peoples believe and why and how that affects their behaviour. Religious literacy matters not because it has the answer to how we can creatively co-exist and govern ourselves, but because religious ignorance breeds bigotry, brutality, and violence.

4

Religion and Contemporary Science

If, as I have been repeating, today's study of theology and religion is not concerned with training people for various ministries in the institutions that practise and even promote faith traditions, but rather is concerned with those who wish to understand the role theology and religion is playing in society, then one of the key subjects to be tackled is that between the scientific and the religious understandings of our world. In university courses, this study is usually in the second and third years when the student has become familiar with how 'religion' might be understood.

In the past, and particularly in Christianity, the relationship between theology and science has been a troubled one. There are classic 'scenes' that are often referred to – like the condemnation of Galileo over his theory (still unproven at that time) of the earth moving around the sun. But historians of science have increasingly demythologized such scenes. Galileo's tempestuous arrogance won him few friends – in the Vatican or elsewhere. And there were many powerful figures in the Catholic Church who themselves accepted the heliocentric view of the cosmos.

Even so, the relationship between theology and science has had a bad press and sometimes it is still staged as a struggle between faith and facts, religious myths and secular reasoning: there are creationists who deny both contemporary work in cosmology and the evolution of the species; there are loud and often uninformed atheistic scientists who see religion as the source of the world's worst violence and the pernicious lingering of a patho-logical delusion. These are the extreme edges of a large and continuing engagement between two modes of examining the ultimate questions, often, in my opinion, with great subtlety. It is an engage-ment, however, that is not without its controversies. Consider, for example, the reaction that greeted the recent election to a fellowship of a theologian on a NASA-sponsored project at Princeton University to examine the implications for human society of discovering life elsewhere in the universe. Given the substantial number of planets found since 1992 circling stars outside our own solar system, and given there are approximately a septillion stars – that's 1 followed by twenty-four noughts – in what is observable of our universe, it is becoming increasingly likely that there are planets out there with water and an atmosphere that can sustain life. But that a Christian theologian should be seconded to help think through the implications for religious faiths (not just Christian ones) of an actual discovery was met by some of the scientific world with incredulity and even hostility.

Certainly, religion and science approach the world differently; they ask different questions. Broadly speaking, science asks the 'how' question: how it is that . . . this is composed? Or, how it is that, given situation A, we might understand situation B? Religions, on the other hand, ask 'why' and 'what': why is it that this happened? And what does this mean? There no final answers such that this approach can be said to be right and that approach wrong. 'God' is certainly not one of the answers easily wielded – as we saw in Chapter 2. For both scientists and people of faith, wrestling to understand is evident. It's a wrestling that issues from a fundamental curiosity human beings seem to have with being alive at all and living in a world they feel they must somehow manage for their flourishing.

It's a wrestling that will never go away because curiosity is of the nature of being human. For both scientists and people of faith, the questions will never end.

Currently, the scientific world is still pursuing Stephen Hawking's quest for a Unified Theory of Everything: how the four forces we know of – gravity, electro-magnetism, strong and weak interactions (which are nuclear at the sub-atomic level, like radioactivity) – interrelate to compose what we might call 'nature' (though its so-called laws are increasingly more like 'stabilities under certain conditions'). There are, though, puzzles emerging. The famous Higgs particle, for example, weighs staggeringly less than it should if it is to 'fulfill its function as the universe's mass-giver', and the energy distributed across empty space, known as the cosmological constant, is '102 orders of magnitude lower than we would expect'.[1]

Scientific inquiry gets feverishly active as these unanswered questions arise. But curiosity is not confined to the sciences. Who is to say how close or how different the febrile intellectual activity in science is to the questions posed by life circum-

[1] Daniel Cossins, 'Truth Before Beauty: Our Universe is Uglier Than We Thought', *New Scientist*, 3 March 2018.

stances that confuse and bewilder those holding to a religious faith? Like human suffering and the all-too-evident experience of human tragedy. 'Mystery' is not a word religions use lightly. The Greek word means 'hidden', and human beings cry out to know, whatever their approach to the fundamental questions of life. We have evolved from and through uncertainty and threat – knowing is our way of stabilizing and predicting things.

But where once there might have been a stand-off between religion and science (even though there are a large number of scientists who are open about their religious allegiance), the world in which we live is dominated with scientific inquiry, and the applications of that inquiry drive the innovative technologies we have grown accustomed to. So the study of theology and religion must foster engagements. The contemporary university (and the funding of research councils internationally) is investing heavily in interdisciplinary projects. The pursuit of answers to what are often termed the 'Big Questions' is recognized as requiring co-operation across faculties and academic disciplines. There are laboratories around the world devoted to investigating the origins of life and attempting to create life or understand the prebiotic conditions that enabled chains of fatty acids and proteins to form membrane walls and self-replicating cells. There are projects in cognitive and neuroscience inquiring into near-death experiences in order to get a clearer understanding of the process of dying. But both the nature of, and questions pertaining to, life and death have deeply religious significance. Birth and death, how one enters and how one leaves this world, are key sites of religious ritual. And we saw that even with our Neanderthal predecessors. The significance of life and death impacts not just socially and politically, but also ethically. It attracts profound and subtle debates within religious faiths about abortion, euthanasia, and the death penalty. These debates have had to accommodate, more recently, advances in science like genome editing and the cloning of species. Courses in the study of theology and religion explicitly examine what is at issue here, where scientific discovery and application meet the values encoded in any faith.

The Body

Meanwhile, the medical sciences are coming to recognize increasingly the effect of practices, mind-states, and habits cultivated within religious pieties; how they impact physical and psychological well-being. The attention to mindfulness and alternative therapies – from meditation to listening to or playing music – comes at a time when neuroscience is making us aware that minds are profoundly embodied. There is ongoing and extensive research into the effect of moods and emotions upon a sense of human flourishing. And, despite the persistent view that religions are concerned more with preparations for the afterlife than with living this one, in fact religions worldwide have always been very much concerned with the body. We can go right back to the early shamans and the pollen controversy from the Introduction. However the pollens got into that grave, all of them are from flowers with known medicinal properties. So shamans may have transcended and shift-shaped through all the material constrictions of this life, but part of their role and respect in the communities that honoured and supported them was as healers and wound-dressers. The elaborate dietary codes, the practices of fasting and even celibacy found in all subsequent religious faiths are as much physiological in their effect as spiritual. In fact, to the extent that it can be said that all religions are concerned broadly with 'salvation', then this word comes directly from the Latin *salus*, which means 'health'.

The word 'spiritual' is another key concept that

any course in the study of theology and religion must examine. It is used to speak of everything from monks in the desert experiencing Satanic visions to hugging trees and speaking to dolphins. As such, it's a slippery eel of a term, especially now when it has been so commercialized and packaged in self-help manuals and scented oils. Its origins lie in the words for 'wind' or 'breath' – as that which enables all life to live. No life was at all possible on this planet until there was oxygen. While the universe is 13.7 billon years old and our galaxy has been giving birth to stars for around 13 billon years, the solar system in which we sit emerged about 4.6 billion years ago, and Earth around 4.5. Unlike Venus, it had a magnetic field, and this field enabled it to develop, and keep the sun from burning off its atmosphere. But the atmosphere had little or no oxygen. For more than 2 billion years the Earth was grey and lifeless, 'wreathed in the mists and organic hazes of those days'.[2] Then came what geologists call the 'Great Oxygenation Event' around 2.4 billion years ago. Now life began to evolve. The word 'spiritual', then, is related to what is most fundamental for our being able to live at all – our ability to breathe.

[2] Jan Zalasiewicz and Mark Williams, *The Goldilocks Planet* (Oxford: Oxford University Press, 2012), p. 28.

In the West, marked from the seventeenth century by Descartes's separation of mind from body, dualistic modes of thinking were cultivated that were mirrored socially and politically in the distinction between the private and the public, religious belief and secular engagement. Theologies were impacted by this dualism. Religious sensibility and conviction was locked into the private domain, the household, of the individual citizen. Freedom became the freedom to choose. In many countries, taxes were reduced and several state institutions privatized so that individual citizens could have more of a say in how they spent the money they earned. In the 1980s, the British Prime Minister, Margaret Thatcher, summed up this social atomism (allied to a new economics of free trade) in her famous remark that there was no such thing as society. Even in the late twentieth century, philosophies of mind could conduct thought experiments in which brains might be placed in vats. Such philosophies could then concentrate on the purely cognitive processes whereby we come to know anything. And the more we understood these processes, the more we could translate and mimic them in the newly conceived computers to develop AI. 'Mind' came to be conceived as a by-product of the electrochemical machinery of our embodied brains.

But the problem of 'mind' didn't go away. Nor was its existence and emergence solved. Neuro- and cognitive science increasingly came to recognize that our intelligence is profoundly emotional, and if it is emotional, then it is embodied. The analogy between mind and computer collapsed and, for a time, scientists at universities like MIT (Massachusetts Institute of Technology) focused on developing 'smart' environments or generic software applications. Various AI 'winters' set in as AI failed on its promise of 'human-level machine intelligence'. Brains in vats became a piece of 1960s sci-fi. The body was back on the agenda, not least in terms of brain research. The new era of AI research opened with notions of 'neural networks' and 'genetic algorithms' whereby machines could learn by experience to progress towards 'brain emulation' and 'biological cognition'. The relationship of organic physiology to 'mind' still remains far from clear, but with the new considerations of our emotional intelligence and how we perceive and experience the world in and through our bodies questions forcefully emerged about religion experience and conviction. As I said in Chapter 1, religion at the time was taking to the streets, internationally. It was no longer socially and politically 'contained' within the mosques, temples, synagogues, and churches. It was going public.

Religion and Contemporary Science

Neuroscience

As the twenty-first century has progressed and religion has gained an increasing presence as a player
on the global stage, and as 'deradicalization' programmes have begun to emerge, the work on emotion
by scientists has expanded. Subjects have emotions,
we have always known that, but these emotions are
communicated and shared. They are even conta-
gious. When one baby cries in a nursery, the other
babies start to cry. This is a common observation
on maternity wards, but it is also a key to empathy
among human beings and a sense of belonging. So
how does this happen? Enter two neurophysiolo-
gists, Giacomo Rizzolatti and Luciano Fadiga at the
University of Parma, who discovered that certain
animals (they were working with monkeys) have
'mirror neurons'. These are triggered in certain circumstances to mimic and reflect the behaviours of
others. The reason I'm not just a passive observer at
a boxing match but wriggling in my seat and jumping
up at a smart left hook, the reason I'm experiencing
something of the same adrenalin rushes and fury as
the contestants, is, in part, down to these neurons
and the endocrinal discharges they trigger.

Meanwhile, it is becoming increasingly evident
to neuroscientists that consciousness is only the

most illuminated part of what is going on in our minds. It accounts for only possibly 10 per cent of our brain activity. Deeper things by far at work: memories, moods, imagination, and beliefs have a much stronger hold on the way we perceive and experience than calculative reasoning does. In 2015, the neuroscientist David Eagleman opened his six-part PBS documentary, *The Brain*, with the question 'What is Reality?' His exploration began by informing the television audience that there is neither light nor sound inside the head: it's dark, dark, dark in the brain. We process light waves and sound waves from a world that is without colour and silent. Every animal does this and every animal's sensory abilities differ. *Homo sapiens* creates colours in response to a spectrum of red to violet waves, but this spectrum, Eagleman informs us, is only capable of responding to one tenth of a trillionth of the waves available out there! We *see as*; we don't just see. If it is important to understand *what* we see, it is equally important to understand *how we see the way we do*.

So what has all this to do with the study of theology and religion – beyond, that is, various attempts to find a 'God gene' that followed from the completion of the genome sequence in 2003? In brief: contemporary science is changing the way we think about ourselves as human beings – how we think about what we are and where we came from – and changing also the way we understand the fabric of the cosmos of which we are a part. This has been a theme right throughout this book: that the exploration in theology and religion is as much an exploration into what it is to be human as any exploration into the nature of 'god'. What we are, where we came from, what are we here for: these are as much theological questions as scientific ones. Courses in religion and science are some of the most popular in the university curriculum, increasingly so, and they are introducing students to these new scientific understandings and raising the theological questions they pose. But the questions posed are not viewed as necessarily anti-thetical to the theological task of faith as it seeks a better understanding of its beliefs and practices. Science is only the enemy of a theological world-view in the eyes of certain fundamentalists.

In 2013, the Dalai Lama (the spiritual leader of Tibetan Buddhists), for example, welcomed new researches into the neuro- and cognitive science of consciousness. He invited teams of such scientists (with all their sophisticated equipment) to the exiled Tibetan Buddhist community in India in order to examine the states of mind that are entered into by monks with long and deep experience of meditation. He has a strong association with the Center for

Ethics and Transformative Values at MIT, now named after him. In 2005 he opened a conference there on 'Investigating the Mind: Exchanges between Buddhism and the Biobehavioral Sciences on How the Mind Works'. Those who practise meditation have a first-hand (sometimes called 'phenomenological') account of different state of consciousness, honed over centuries by former practitioners. The scientist doing brain scans using fMRI (functional magnetic resonance imaging) and PET (positron emission tomography) technology examines these different states empirically. We are back to the 'insider' and the 'outsider' and how both perspectives are necessary for the most detailed accounts of understanding religious experience. The Dalai Lama spoke of certain Buddhist experiences of 'luminous consciousness' and 'pure awareness' that must have some sort of physical basis correlating with patterns of brain activity. In 2013, he taught a complete session in the centre at MIT on 'The Stages of Meditation', available in several parts on YouTube. As our material condition, which cannot be divorced from the material conditions of the cosmos itself, is more deeply explored by science, the study of theology and religion is learning, not uncritically. It is incorporating the insights of science and adding its own to scientific inquiry.

Religion and Contemporary Science

For Buddhists, consciousness goes all the way down, and that poses a question to neuro- and cognitive science. Scientists can plumb the various electro-chemical wavelengths beneath waking states and even states of sleep and dreaming. But when human beings enter sleep and REM states associated with dreaming, then they seem to lose consciousness. REM stands for rapid eye movement and this accompanies dream activity in the brain. But what happens below, in so-called 'non-REM', when the brain is still functioning but its electro-chemical activity registers in slow delta waves? We enter the realm of the sleepwalkers, and sudden arousal from this level of sleep can have violent, primitive reactions. Sleepwalkers have murdered and raped; they have also driven cars and gone shopping. The brain processes behind sleepwalking are still a mystery. So do Buddhist practices of meditation actually allow access to levels of deep mindfulness that science has yet to examine?

Cosmology – and Our Place in It

Science is also posing for the study of theology and religion the question of where human beings fit into this world of particle physics and molecular biology. Most religions (particularly the Abrahamic faiths of Judaism, Christianity, and Islam) have being human as some summit of the Creator's achievement. We are given a special place in the great chain of being. To go back to the concerns and controversies about the heliocentric universe: it was not so much the idea that the earth revolved around the sun, rather than the sun and planets revolving around the earth, that was controversial. The difficulty was not just perceptual – surely the sun rose and set upon the earth. The difficulty was also theological: this perception *demonstrated* that human beings were at the centre of divine creation. But to understand that our solar system lies in a remote and quiet corner of one of the spiral arms of the Milky Way – a galaxy itself over a hundred light years in diameter and only one of a cluster of fifty-four such galaxies in this part of the universe (with the Andromeda galaxy far larger than our own) – dislodges the human species from any exalted religious prominence. We are not at all the centre of anything. Even our planet is not the centre of anything (if, indeed, the expanding universe can even be said to have a centre).

Furthermore, it's not simply that we have knowledge now that the Neanderthals who came before us, and with whom we interbred, lacked. The *Homo* species had a long prehistory in which several different varieties of *Homo* became extinct. Having separated from our ape cousins 6 million years ago, there have been recognizable *Homo*s going back more than 2.2 million years.

The study of theology and religion cannot ignore the findings of science, for these are findings about creation itself. So it must ask what these discoveries mean in the light of faith's different accounts of creation, and beliefs both in a divine Creator and in ourselves – what these discoveries mean, that is, for the different sacred texts and how we interpret them. It must ask what they mean for an understanding of ourselves as part of a vast creation. And this isn't just about where we came from and where we are heading. It's also about what, if anything, is significant in our being here at all. The questions are crucial, because the various world faiths have views on these penultimate matters.

There is a paradox, and that means a tension, at the heart of the Abrahamic faiths. Humankind was fashioned, according to the Hebrew Bible informing those faiths, from the dust of the earth (*'adamah* in Hebrew). But the mythic figure of Adam was God's final creation on the sixth and last day of His activity. Humankind alone was formed 'in the image and likeness' of God to tend and steward the rest

111

of creation. Psalm 8 establishes humankind's status in a cosmological setting. The opening and closing verses of the psalm frame that status with 'Lord our sovereign'. The psalm then details the creation of the heavens and the earth, and a cosmology into which humankind is inserted:

> You have made them little lower than the angels
>   and crowned them with glory and honor.
> You made them rulers over the works of your
>   hands; you put everything under their feet. (vv.
>   5–6)

Yet the exaltation of the human as the centre and pinnacle of the created order is always in tension to a submission necessary to the sovereignty of God. There lies the paradox of the human who is free to be as he or she is only in obedience.

There is, then, in the Abrahamic tradition, and this observation extends to other world faiths like Hinduism and Buddhism, a continual appeal to human beings to transcend their limitations and participate in the divine. At the same time, and maybe more in the Abrahamic faiths than the Eastern religions, the created order is conceived with humans at its heart. And that anthropocentrism is challenged by what science is observing about the nature of the cosmos. It is even further challenged by the notion of other planets outside the solar system on which life may be found. Hence NASA's legitimate inclusion of a theologian on their Princeton project, despite lawsuits. The encounter with alien life elsewhere in this or any other possible universe raises profound questions for the traditional teachings of many world faiths. But the challenges don't necessarily destroy religious faith – maybe (and in a way that might challenge the scientific world) because too many resonate with that reply given by my Sikh graduate student in the class I mentioned in Chapter 2: the experience on the ground is, 'It works.'

Blade Runner 2049

And that observation enables us to reverse the questioning: in what ways might theology and religion inform science? The response to this even thirty years ago would have been one of ridicule: the world-views of each were so different as to be just speaking past each other. In 1959, in a hugely influential lecture delivered at the University of Cambridge, the novelist C.P. Snow lamented the divide between the arts and the sciences, in part heralding the triumph of scientific reason. It was called *The Two Cultures and the Scientific Revolution* and in it Snow argued that the cultures could never meet because one was on the decline while the other was on its way to international acclaim. He spoke of the need for 'bridges', and certainly, over the last sixty years, bridges from the humanities to the sciences have been painstakingly constructed. But is the study of theology and religion included here, and have the bridges only been built from one side?

I would argue there has been an expansion of the scientific world into the arts. Recall, particularly, technology's impact upon the development of new media (from interactive gaming in virtual reality to the computer-generated special effects that no block-buster movie can do without). If the German father of sociology, Max Weber, spoke of the disenchantment of the world in the wake of the Industrial Revolution and the rise of instrumental reason, then the re-enchantment is being led by advances in technological science.

So what about the impact of theology and religion on the sciences? I would argue this is and remains profound, though at the time that Snow was lecturing, a wave of neo-orthodox Protestantism, circling around the Swiss theologian Karl Barth, was decrying all association with 'natural theology'. While not counter-cultural, this wave did cut off at the knees any theological rapprochement with culture.

114

Nevertheless, to return to my claim of the impact of theology and religion on the sciences, let's approach this by looking at a recent film: Denis Villeneuve's *Blade Runner 2049* (2017). The plot of the film issues from a 'miracle' – a child born from a human being and a replicant. A replicant is an AI agent, biologically engineered in the laboratories of the Wallace Corporation. A blade runner is an agent trained to track down and 'retire' outdated models. Blade runner K (played by Ryan Gosling), who is also a replicant, stands before the desk of his boss, Lieutenant Joshi (played by Robin Wright), in the Los Angeles Police Department. He informs her about his discovery of the child's existence. She orders him to kill it. There is a huge wall, she tells him, separating human beings from replicants, and this wall must be maintained or chaos will ensue.[3] But she detects a resistance in K that seems irrational. After all, he's 'retired' any number of replicants before. 'Are you refusing me?' she asks him, challenging him to vocalize a resistance to a murder he's unable to explain. But the child and its

---

[3] Nick Bostrom, Director of the Future of Humanity Institute at the University of Oxford, calls this 'chaos' 'existential catastrophe', because it puts into question the very essence of human nature (particularly, its supremacy). See Nick Bostrom, *Superintelligence: Paths, Dangers, Strategies* (Oxford: Oxford University Press, 2014).

potential murder seems to trigger a new level of AI self-awareness in K beyond his programming. 'To be born is to have a soul, I guess,' K explains. He's never killed someone with a soul, someone who was born, before. The soul, philosophically, from Aristotle onwards, is the life-force animating the body. Replicants only have synthetically manufactured bodies.

There is no explicit theology or religion as such in the world of *Blade Runner 2049*, just there is no nature and all the trees are dead. But religious themes run through the plot like the engineered plasma down the veins of a replicant. Two are prominent in the scene I have described: the miraculous birth and the soul. And both are related to types of birth – of a girl, and, more obliquely, of the possibility for the soul of life after death. Love, a superior and named replicant, is called 'the best angel of all'.

What is going on here? What is this film giving cultural expression to? Why even appeal to religious language? I would put this down to what some have called 'cultural memory' and 'cultural imagination'. 'Cultural memory' is what, in the long and intricate history of human civilizations, remains stored up in great collective archives of images, myths, incidents, figures (real and imaginary), and past ways of living. 'Cultural imagination' is the activation of this archive at any one given time in a particular creative expression – like a film or a novel or even an academic treatise. *Blade Runner 2049*, like its predecessor *Blade Runner* (1982), offers an inquiry into what it is that makes human beings a distinctive species. We're back with the grand question: what am I? – a question as fundamental to all religions as the question about the nature and character of the divine. To borrow the famous title of a 1933 book by the psychologist Carl Jung, the film concerns 'modern man in search of a soul'. And the use of the word 'soul' is interesting. It returns us to those questions in philosophy, neuroscience, and cognitive science about the nature of mind and whence it emerges, and how. In Greek, 'soul' is '*psyche*' – from which we get psychology and psychiatry. But, for some reason, in *Blade Runner 2049*, 'soul' was more appropriate to the screenwriters than 'mind' or 'consciousness' because the depth of its mythic resonance belongs to a specific person – the child of a replicant and a former blade runner (Deckard, played by Harrison Ford). 'Soul' bestows a certain sacred dignity upon those who are born with one – rather like being made in the image and likeness of God. At one point in the plot K even believes he might be the child and therefore have a 'soul'. But then he discovers this is not so. Nevertheless, the film makes clear that he does have a 'soul' – for he is able to empathize and creatively imagine, despite the fact that all his memories are manufactured implants and his range of emotions is programmed. He develops emotional intelligence beyond the specifications of his model. At the end of the film, K sacrifices himself to bring together the father (Deckard) and the child, now grown into a young woman (Stelline, played by Carla Juri), and he dies from his wounds in peace.

The film, then, gives this religious language a new currency and relevance. We are not talking about the past here as a 'cultural memory' when that memory is reactivated for the present and future cultural imagination. The language of the 'soul' is back on the cultural agenda – it is no longer just a genre of pop music.

Between the Animal and the Angel

After more than one and half centuries of thinking through evolution and following in the wake of the landmark Human Genome Project, we are recognizing that human beings are profoundly related to all other living species past and present. We, too, are animals, as animals were once molluscs and molluscs were once microbial life. It should come as no surprise, then, that the question has arisen as to whether other animals are religious. How far down the chain of being does the religious response to being alive go?

Enter the primatologist Jane Goodall, working in the Gombe National Park in Tanzania:

In the Kakombe valley is a magnificent waterfall. There is a great roar as the water cascades down through the soft green air from the stream bed some eighty feet above. Over countless aeons the water has worn a perpendicular groove in the sheer rock. Ferns move ceaseless in the wind creating by the falling water, and vines hang down on either side. For me, it is a magical place, and a spiritual one. And sometimes, as they approach, the chimpanzees display in slow, rhythmic motion along the river bed. They pick up and throw great rocks and branches. They leap to seize the hanging vines, and swing out over the stream in the spray-drenched wind until it seems the slender stems must snap or be torn from their lofty moorings.

For ten minutes or more they may perform this magnificent 'dance'. Why? Is it not possible that the chimpanzees are responding to some feeling like awe? A feeling generatcd by the mystery of the water that seems alive, always rushing past yet never going, always the same yet ever different.[4]

Goodall is not alone in asking the question about animal religion, and raising it here, in my concluding remarks on religion and science, is more about the ongoing quest to understand the distinctiveness of *Homo sapiens* than about supporting its possibility. In some ways, investigations into what might be described as religious behaviour in animals mark one of the outer limits in the study of theology and religion. AI marks another of those limits – though the more I read about what is called 'super-intelligence' or the 'transhuman' or the 'post-human', and the more I watch TV series like *Westworld*, then the more, like the screenwriters of *Blade Runner 2049*, I think of the religious treatises on angels. The religious imagination is very far from obsolete – it is utterly inseparable from all our understandings about and aspirations for what we are and might be.

[4] Jane Goodall (with Philip Berman), *Reason for Hope: A Spiritual Journey* (New York: Soko Publications, 1999), pp. 188–9.

Conclusion

In the recent BBC series *Civilizations* (2018), there is not one episode in which a religion fails to appear – from shamanism to Catholicism. In a dramatic instalment called 'Radiance', the commentator Simon Schama examines a shift in the work of the Spanish painter Francisco de Goya (1746–1828) and the dark madnesses that overwhelm his canvases following the violent conquest of Spain by Napoleon. After centuries of glorious colour and inventive design, inspired by both Islam and Catholic Christianity, religion, too, has been eclipsed it seems. An endless, voiceless howling is evident in the gaping mouths and livid eyes of Goya's human figures. Viewing one of Goya's late paintings, *The Dog*, Schama comments that civilization (in terms of painting, shape, light, rhythm, and the natural world) has been reduced to a mangy mongrel head peering over a desolate mound of earth into the murky chaos of a threatening storm. The despair and nihilism of the work are palpable. The Byzantine golds have turned to ochres. Without illumination, without form, without hope, civilization faces its demise. That world is recreated in Denis Villeneuve's *Blade Runner 2049*, and only artificial intelligence can live in it.

Every civilization we know of had and has political and religious foundations. Sometimes they have worked together, sometimes they have worked in parallel, and sometimes they have worked against each other. But there's no likelihood either will disappear if any civilized world is to remain. So thinking through the relationship between religion and culture, understanding what it is human beings are responding to in being religious and practising a piety, is fundamental. Atheists may shout loud and raw about the historical association of religion with violence. No one can deny the facts, though no secular nation state can raise clean hands. However, atheists are faced with an impossible task. It's easy to denounce on the evidence from history, and scepticism (about the existence of the gods, true knowledge, or reality itself) has a long tradition. But it remains impossible to prove God *doesn't exist* – whatever is understood by and named as 'God'. All the scales of probability (and mathematics) are human scales; far too human, religious faiths would say.

The student studying theology and religion is rather like the sixteenth-century Spanish conquistador Hernán Cortés, not an innocent man by any means and bearing within him any number of conflicting interests. And this little book, too, is threaded with any number of my own interests (and limitations). But consider here John Keats's poem 'On First Looking Into Chapman's Homer', in which he imagines Cortés stepping intrepidly into his newly discovered world:

> He star'd at the Pacific – and all his men
> Look'd at each other with a wild surmise –
> Silent, upon a peak in Darien.

Students of theology and religion are not out for conquest (and the land Cortés 'discovered' was already well known to all those who already occupied it), but the same stunned awe, curiosity, and, sometimes, simply silence is necessary before the unexplained and inexplicable. Because however the divine might be understood and experienced, the study of theology and religion is staring also into the profundities of who *we* are.

We're back at the mouth of the Shanidar cave in the Zagros Mountains.

Further Reading

Introduction

Dimitra Papagianni and Michael A. Morse, *The Neanderthals Rediscovered: How Modern Science is Rewriting Their Story* (London: Thames & Hudson, 2015).

Thomas Tweed, *Crossing and Dwelling: A Theory of Religion* (Cambridge, MA: Harvard University Press, 2006).

A Millennial Age

Callum G. Brown, *The Death of Christian Britain: Understanding Secularism, 1800–2000* (London: Routledge, 2009).

Gilles Kepel, *The Revenge of God: The Resurgence of Islam, Christianity and Judaism in the Modern World* (Cambridge: Polity, 1994).

Further Reading

Living with Invisibility

Graham Ward, *Unimaginable: What We Imagine and What We Can't* (London: I.B. Tauris, 2018).

Religion and Power

William T. Cavanaugh, *The Myth of Religious Violence* (Oxford: Oxford University Press, 2009).

Michael Kirwan, *Political Theology: An Introduction* (London: SCM Press, 2009).

Scott M. Thomas *The Global Resurgence of Religion and the Transformation of International Relations: The Struggle for the Soul of the Twenty-First Century* (New York: Palgrave Macmillan, 2005).

Religion and Contemporary Science

Nick Bostrom, *Superintelligence: Paths, Dangers, Strategies* (Oxford: Oxford University Press, 2014).

Allan Chapman, *Slaying the Dragons: Destroying Myths in the History of Science and Faith* (Oxford: Lion Books, 2013).

Antonio Damasio, *The Feeling of What Happens: Body, Emotion, and the Making of Consciousness* (London: Vintage Books, 2000).

Evan Thompson, *Waking, Dreaming, Being* (New York: Columbia University Press, 2015).

Index

Index

Index